KICKSTART YOUR BOOK

KICKSTART YOUR BOOK

A Guide to Estimating, Designing, Printing, and Shipping
Your Crowdfunded Publishing Project

BY DON LEEPER

Tasora
Minneapolis

 Published in the United States by Tasora Books.

Print ISBN: 978-1-949793-98-7
Ebook ISBN: 978-1-949793-90-1

DISTRIBUTED BY
Itasca Books
5120 Cedar Lake Road
Minneapolis, Minnesota 55416

https://www.itascabooks.com/

PRODUCED BY BOOKMOBILE
https://www.bookmobile.com

All photographs by Cory Ryan, CT Ryan Photography, unless otherwise credited.

TABLE OF CONTENTS

ACKNOWLEDGMENTS

Many thanks to Jessica Knight of Modern Writing Services (modernwritingservices.com) for shaping an unwieldy collection of blog posts into an actual book. Also thanks to the great crew here at Bookmobile, who helped me avoid putting my foot in my mouth on technical matters too often. The usual assignment of blame pertains.

PREFACE

CROWDFUNDING IS THE BETTER WAY TO PUBLISH INDEPENDENTLY

If you're an indie publisher, artist, or organization interested in publishing a book, crowdfunding is the way to go, unless you're already a traditional publisher with long-established industry resources. The list of advantages to crowdfunding is long and comprehensive, crowned by the fact that when you crowdfund, you do the marketing for your book *before* you print it. Don't get me wrong: mounting a crowdfunding campaign is a lot of work. But it's no more work than marketing after printing, with the added benefit that you have a much better idea of how many books to print. Other benefits of crowdfunded publishing include:

- You publish on *your* schedule: you're not locked into rigid book industry publishing schedules and multi-year lead times.
- There's no requirement to sell thousands of copies to make your book a success: depending on specific costs of publishing your book, you can pay for its production by rounding up as few as 250 backers. Compare this with traditional publishing, where selling 3,000 copies is the rule of thumb for a minimal breakeven.
- Because you are connecting with your audience—your backers—directly, you receive more dollars per book and can produce exactly the book you want, unrestricted by the tiny financial return on selling a book through the traditional book industry, with its multiple layers of middlemen.

Interestingly, while crowdfunding is the newest wrinkle in book publishing, it is also one of the oldest. Beginning in the 17th century, selling subscriptions to a new book was a common way of financing it's production. For example, John James Audubon financed the meticulous engraving and hand-coloring of his magisterial *The Birds of America* by selling subscriptions in the United Kingdom; and the first illustrated edition of Milton's *Paradise Lost*, published by the prominent London publisher Jacob Tonson, had a subscriber list of over 500 people. So the model has a long and storied history.

While crowdfunding resolves a lot of the challenges in independent publishing, some remain. One is the need to bootstrap your knowledge of book printing sufficiently so that when you get the first copies of your book back from the printer, it is exactly what you expected and wanted. Traditional publishers have experienced staff navigating the myriad choices available in papers, printing technologies, and bindings. These folks are used to working with the requirements of book printers. While there is no need for you to learn all the ins and outs of book printing, you need to know at least the basics, and you'll want to know how to use printing techniques to make your book special.

That's the purpose of this book.

How do I know this stuff? I've spent 20 years operating a successful short-run digital book printing company, Bookmobile, that provides services to some of the best independent publishers in the country (as well as increasing numbers of crowdfunded publishing projects). And it's based not just on my experience, but the experience of our staff. Perhaps more importantly, it's also based on my 10 years of personal experience buying offset printing for book publishers prior to founding Bookmobile's digital print service. (More on the differences between offset, short-run digital, and print-on-demand printing later.) Further, I started a traditional publishing company, Culpepper Press, with three partners, and so have first-hand experience of the processes of traditional publishing, from editing and design through printing, distribution, and paying royalties. So there's a lot of collective wisdom and experience represented here, with the hope of benefiting people new to the game.

Crowdfunded publishing and the freedom it gives creators is the most exciting thing to happen to independent publishing in my career. Take advantage of it to make your creation real!

INTRODUCTION

CROWDFUNDING VS. TRADITIONAL BOOK PUBLISHING

The traditional method of publishing books is risky, full of obstacles, and expensive. But by using a crowdfunding model and doing your homework to determine the best printing options for your project, you can get all the benefits of traditional publishing, with much less risk—and conceivably even earn a profit.

The process of mounting a crowdfunding campaign combines both fundraising and, equally if not more importantly, marketing. The hardest part of publishing is always reaching your audience, but Kickstarter and other crowdfunding sites offer a new way to do this. In addition, the crowdfunding model of funding and distribution enables creators to incorporate book design elements that work poorly with the standard publishing model because of distribution issues: fancy embossed covers, custom cover stocks, rich color printing, and more.

This book is for crowdfunding creators who are producing books via the crowdfunding model, whether those books be art books, photography books, comics, novels, poetry, nonfiction, eBooks, or even components of a game package. We'll cover topics relevant to any book publisher—design, printing, distribution—as well as crowdfunding-specific topics such as creating a project budget and how to fulfill your backer rewards.

THE CHALLENGES OF TRADITIONAL BOOK PUBLISHING

The traditional way of publishing books is risky because it entails selling through the book trade—the network connecting publishers to the distributors, wholesalers, and booksellers that get print books into the hands of consumers in the United States—which requires giving huge discounts off the list price to those entities. A publisher is lucky to get 40 percent of the list price for each sale after all the middlemen take their cuts. This would not be so bad in itself, if it were not for the fact that all sales are returnable. So while a publisher may get orders for 1,000 books, only a fraction of those will actually sell to consumers. The rest will be returned for credit. On average, over 30 percent of books shipped are returned. Publishers still have to pay for printing those books, for shipping them, and, ultimately, for disposing of them instead of paying to store them. To add insult to injury, returned books are often shopworn and therefore cannot be sold as new.

The only printing strategy that makes sense in these circumstances is to print enough copies so that the printing cost per copy is very low—low enough that you might, hypothetically, make some money. That generally means printing way more books than you need and, for color books, printing in the Far East to lower costs—which adds the risk of long lead times for reprints, should the book take off.

When Amazon entered the fray, the situation got better in the sense that audiences can now find books more readily, but got much worse because of Amazon's discounting. Amazon uses books as loss leaders to build strength across all retail categories, putting enormous pressure on physical bookstores and devaluing books across the board. Amazon actively encourages showrooming, with software enabling people browsing in a bookstore to comparison shop and order directly from their mobile device. The consequence is that the bookstore foots the bill for the inviting space in which to browse while Amazon reaps the sales. For categories in which the visual and physical attributes of the book are the main selling points, such as art books, this showrooming is deadly: stores cannot afford to display a book if consumers are just going to buy it from Amazon, which sells expensive books at prices no physical bookstore can match. The result is that museum stores and other venues that used to carry good selections of art books can't afford to any more. If people can't see and handle these books they won't buy them, and whole categories of books suffer.

THE CROWDFUNDING ALTERNATIVE

Crowdfunding offers a new way to engage readers while also mitigating the risks of traditional publishing. Sites such as Kickstarter enable you to reach out to your existing fans as well as promote to new fans in the process of raising money to publish your book. You figure out how much your project will cost, set a fundraising goal, and mount a campaign to reach out to existing and new fans asking them to donate to your project. Those who donate are called backers. Typically for a crowdfunded project, you promise rewards to your backers; in the case of a book project, this is usually a signed copy of the book recognizing their contribution. A successful campaign raises enough money to print enough books so that you can send them to your backers as well as sell extras through other venues, such as your website and online marketplaces. (The question of whether to sell through traditional book trade channels is a complicated one that we'll discuss later). Here's a brief step-by-step outline of a publishing project using this model:

1. DESIGN YOUR BOOK.

While you may be able to raise money by crowdfunding before you have a book ready to print, doing so will significantly reduce your credibility to funders. Also, without having the book designed, you can't accurately price printing and shipping costs, which are crucial for setting your funding goal. While artistic concerns are obviously central to the design process, don't ignore the impact that design choices have on production costs. Identify and work with a good book printer early on to avoid expensive pitfalls and get the best quality book possible.

2. CREATE YOUR PROJECT BUDGET.

You have to know how much your project is going to cost in order to set your fundraising campaign goal. With at least the basic specifications of your book determined—page size, number of pages, type of binding, color or black-and-white printing—you can find out how much your book will cost to print by requesting quotes from printers. Don't forget to add in the other costs of your campaign, including creating a campaign video, keeping track of backers, and fulfilling your backer rewards.

3. PLAN AND EXECUTE YOUR CROWDFUNDING CAMPAIGN.

A successful crowdfunding campaign requires both good planning and good execution. It's a lot of work: writing copy, creating a video, answering questions, pitching funders. But selling through the traditional book trade takes a lot of work, too, with much more risk and much lower potential return.

4. PRINT YOUR BOOK AND FULFILL BACKER REWARDS.

With a successful crowdfunding campaign, most of the financial stress of ordering book printing is eliminated. Some book printers can fulfill your backer rewards as well as print the books—and even act as an ongoing fulfillment service for selling additional copies of your books from your website, events, or as an Amazon merchant.

The chapters that follow cover everything you need to know to plan and execute a successful crowdfunded publishing project. Here's some of what's covered in the book:

- How to set your crowdfunding funding goal.
- What you need to know about book printing before you design your book or have it designed.
- What your options are for designing and laying out your book cover and pages.
- What your options are for printing your book, including print-on-demand, short-run digital printing, and offset.
- How to get pricing from book printers.
- How to prepare images for printing.
- How to prepare your layout files for printing.
- Why printer's proofs are your friend, and how to review and check them.
- What to watch out for in fulfilling your backer rewards.
- How to create and distribute eBooks.

Mounting a crowdfunding campaign to publish a book is no small task, but with good planning (and, of course, a brilliant book), a crowdfunded publishing project has a far better chance of success than one that goes through traditional channels. If you want proof, just browse through Kickstarter's successful projects to see the innumerable books that have been brought to life this way. Then, read on to get started!

CHAPTER I

CREATING A BUDGET

As we noted in the introduction, it's important to design your book *before* you try to create a budget for a crowdfunded publishing project, because the specifics of the end product will dictate production and shipping costs, which vary enormously. But we're starting with an overview of the budgeting process because it's a useful way to get a sense for the big-picture considerations you'll need to keep in mind at every stage.

It's no surprise that creating an accurate budget is important. Your fundraising goal should be set at a level that will look reasonable to potential backers, but you don't want the project to fail because you underestimate the real costs. Book publishers have a very useful tool for addressing just these questions: the Title Profit & Loss worksheet, which is created for each new book the publisher is considering publishing. These P&Ls lend themselves well to creating a crowdfunding budget, with appropriate modifications. Here's an overview of the Title P&L and why it's useful.

THE TITLE P&L

Because book publishers have limited capital to invest in book projects, they examine the income potential for each new book prior to publication. If they don't do this, they go out of business, because they publish too many books that lose money. It's just that simple. This applies to both for-profit and nonprofit publishers—regardless of whether the capital comes from sales or donations or both, it is always limited. The Title P&L is publishers' primary mechanism for evaluating a new book's potential. Title P&Ls are built in five sections: 1) Sales estimates 2) Income, 3) Cost of goods sold, 4) Overhead, and 5) Net profit (or loss). To arrive at the net profit is simple arithmetic:

Income - Cost of goods sold - Overhead = Net profit.

For the purposes of modifying the Title P&L for a crowdfunded publishing project, it makes sense to tweak the standard terminology a bit, because of the following:

- You may very well be putting your project together as an individual or as a one-time collaboration rather than as an established organization with ongoing expenses, so instead of "Overhead," call fixed expenses "Project expenses."
- Book publishing profits are highly sensitive to the number of books sold, so it is useful to strictly segregate costs that vary with the number of books sold, like printing and freight, from one-time costs like cover design. These kinds of costs are called "Cost of goods sold," but to be crystal clear, call them "Variable costs."
- Net profit may not be exactly the right term, because you may very well not be in this for profit. Call it "Surplus" instead, or "Shortfall" if it is a negative number.

So here's the bones of a simplified Title P&L modified for a crowdfunded project:

Income - Variable costs - Project expenses = Surplus (or Shortfall).

THE TITLE P&L, MODIFIED FOR A CROWDFUNDED PROJECT

Here's a simplified Title P&L with hypothetical numbers plugged in. Explanations of each item follow. This example assumes that distribution is limited to your backers and your own direct sales.

BOOK SALES

In this simplified Title P&L, books are only sold directly by you in person or through your website. No-revenue copies for backers and staff are also included here, because doing so facilitates keeping track of total number of copies required.

INCOME

Income is all the money coming into the project, including the book sales income calculated above and your Kickstarter funding. Kickstarter's fees and credit card processing fees are shown as negatives in the Income section because those will reduce the total amount of cash you have to work with right off the bat.

VARIABLE COSTS

Variable costs are all those costs that theoretically vary with how many books you sell and ship.

PRINTING

Printing is tricky to estimate because the cost per book depends partly on how many books you print in a run. On one hand, you don't want to print too few at a time and see your printing cost per book go too high; but on the other hand, you don't want to sink money into printing books that will never sell or otherwise be distributed. Book publishers face this dilemma all the time: they never know how many copies of a book are going to sell (and therefore how many to print). Crowdfunding actually makes the process a bit more rational, because you can estimate up front how many copies to give to backers based on your fundraising target and estimated average donation amounts. (Kickstarter has lots of data about average donation amounts and other stats—see https://www.kickstarter.com/help/stats.) See chapter 4 for more information about getting printing estimates.

SHIPPING MATERIALS

Check out online catalogs such as Uline (https://www.uline.com/) for pricing. If you use a fulfillment service (see below), shipping materials will be included in the fulfillment fee.

SHIPPING/POSTAGE

You can estimate these by using the USPS (https://www.usps.com/nationalpremieraccounts/calculaterates.htm) or UPS (https://wwwapps.ups.com/ctc) websites with an estimate of the book's weight. See appendix A for information about how to estimate a book's weight. And err on the high side here: it is very easy to underestimate shipping costs—especially for international shipping!

TITLE PROFIT & LOSS

Book Sales	Copies	Shipments	Sales
Copies sold to individuals at $45.00	200	0	9,000.00
S&H charged to individuals at $5.00	0	200	1,000.00
Copies given to backers at $0.00	600	0	0.00
S&H for backer copies at $0.00	0	600	0.00
Project copies for creator/team	20	0	0.00
Totals	820	800	10,000.00
Income			**Sales**
Book sales income			10,000.00
Kickstarter funding			24,000.00
Kickstarter fee (5%)			(1,200.00)
Card processing fee (3%–5%)			(960.00)
Total Income			**$31,840.00**

Variable Costs	Copies	Price	Sales
Printing, books sold	200	@ $25.00	5,000.00
Printing, backer and team copies	620	@ $25.00	15,500.00
Shipping, books sold	200	@ $2.65	530.00
Shipping, backer copies	600	@ $2.65	1,590.00
Fulfillment services	800	@ $2.00	1,600.00
Credit card fees on sales at 4%			400.00
Total Variable Costs			**$24,620.00**
Gross Margin			**$7,220.00**

Project Expenses	Sales
Development	
Editorial	250.00
Artwork	50.00
Cover design	700.00
Text design and layout	1,100.00
Printing setup charges	120.00
Travel	50.00
Equipment rental	50.00
Marketing and Promotion	
Project website	500.00

Project Expenses (con't)	**Sales**
Copywriting	125.00
Launch party	400.00
Miscellaneous	200.00
Fundraising	
Video—script	400.00
Video—production	1,000.00
Still photography	400.00
Copywriting	250.00
Professional Services	
Legal	1,000.00
Bookkeeping and accounting	200.00
Tax preparation	200.00
Total Project Expenses	**$6,995.00**

PROJECT SURPLUS (SHORTFALL)	**$225.00**

FULFILLMENT SERVICES

There are companies that provide pick, pack, and ship services at reasonable cost. See chapter 5 for more information on fulfillment options.

CREDIT CARD FEES

It is probably wise to assume that people will be paying you with a credit or debit card. Square (https://squareup.com/) is handy for small organizations and projects.

GROSS MARGIN

Gross margin is Income minus Variable costs. In a classic Title P&L, this can be useful in determining how many books you need to sell to break even. For a crowdfunded book, this shows the number of backers you need to break even.

PROJECT EXPENSES

Project expenses are those things that are necessary whether you sell one book or one million. The cover design, for example, only needs to be done once. Note that the above example includes fundraising expenses, so that the budget really covers the period prior to crowdfunding as well as after.

SURPLUS (OR SHORTFALL)

Surplus (or Shortfall) is what's left after all the costs and expenses are subtracted from the income. Obviously, it can be a positive (Surplus) or negative (Shortfall). Beware: a project surplus does not equal cash flow! This Title P&L shows the surplus (or shortfall) at the completion of the whole project. The numbers can work beautifully in this kind of projection, yet you can still have periods in the middle of the project where your cash outlay is more than your cash coming in. Two things can help make sure this doesn't happen: 1) set your fundraising minimum to cover all anticipated Variable costs and Project expenses, and 2) break out your cash flow month by month, showing money coming in from all sources and all money going out.

There are no doubt items in this sample Title P&L that aren't relevant to your project, and probably relevant items that are missing. See appendix B for a Title P&L worksheet, which can be easily modified to fit your project in Excel, Apple Numbers, or any other spreadsheet program.

The great thing about worksheets is that you can try all kinds of scenarios with different selling prices, sales quantities, fundraising goals, and so on. However, there are two seriously bad things about worksheets:

1. It is extremely easy to have an error in a formula that is hard to detect without systematically checking all formulae in the worksheet. Make sure to double-check all formulae!
2. It is extremely easy to fool yourself by building a plan based on a worksheet with too-optimistic sales or cost assumptions. (This is the bitter voice of experience speaking here!) You have to be optimistic or you wouldn't do a crowdfunding project to begin with, but strive for realistic assumptions and ways to minimize risks.

Do your research and use the best numbers you can in the worksheet—the numbers in the worksheet are not meant to represent reality, though in some cases they may not be far off.

TACKLING THE BOOK TRADE IN A TITLE P&L

Selling through traditional wholesale book channels complicates the Title P&L in ways that are discussed in chapter 5, where we cover fulfillment and distribution. But if you are interested in selling to bookstores, appendix B includes a

Title P&L for selling through the traditional book trade, so you can get a picture of how it works. First, however, read chapter 5 for a bit about the perils of selling to bookstores. It's not necessarily something you shouldn't consider, but if you do, it's best to know clearly what you're getting into.

CHAPTER 2

DESIGNING YOUR BOOK

Now that you've got a sense for the big-picture considerations for a crowdfunded publishing project from start to finish via a budget template, here's the first place to really dig in with your project: designing the book. Remember, *you can't set an accurate budget until you've designed your book.* And while it might seem counterintuitive, you actually need to decide what kind of book *printer* best fits your project best before you begin designing. This is because the choice of design methods and tools partly depends on the kind of printer you use.

CHOOSING WHICH TYPE OF PRINTER TO USE

There are three types of book printers: print-on-demand (POD), short-run digital (SRDP), and offset. Chapter 3 discusses these options in more detail, but here's a quick explanation of the differences:

1. **POD PRINTERS** are best for runs of fewer than 50 copies where limited or no customization is desired, and where you are willing to give up the professional proof approval cycle that is standard to SRDP and offset printing and enables you to control the print quality to the utmost degree. POD printers typically provide free design tools for download or in some cases for use in a web browser. Because of their significant limitations in terms of design capacity and print quality, POD services aren't the best choice for serious publishing projects.

ISBNS AND BARCODES

The ISBN (International Standard Book Number) is the code used to identify specific books or specific editions of books. Look on the back of any book sold in bookstores and you'll see one, accompanied by a barcode. Here's an example ISBN—the one for this book!

978-1-934690-71-0

The left-hand part of the ISBN identifies the country of publication and the publisher. This enables anyone in the book trade to identify the source of the book and therefore where to order it. The right-hand part minus the last digit identifies the particular book. The last digit is a check digit used by computers to confirm that the ISBN has been correctly scanned or keyed in.

The ISBN is in ubiquitous use in libraries and among book publishers, wholesalers and retailers (the traditional book trade). When books are published by traditional publishers, they provide the ISBNs. If you're crowdfunding and self-publishing, you don't need an ISBN for your book unless you want to sell it through the book trade, in which case you absolutely do.

IF—AND ONLY IF—YOU NEED AN ISBN

Again, you don't need an ISBN or barcode for your crowdfunded book if you are only sending it to backers or selling it directly to people yourself. If you want to sell in bookstores or anywhere else that commonly sells books, here's the scoop.

Options for buying an ISBN:

1. Buy from Bowker (https://www.bowker.com/products/ISBN-US.html) or your country's ISBN agency (there's a list on the Wikipedia International Standard Book Number page.) You can buy a single ISBN, or groups of 10, 100, or 1,000. Note that if you create more than one edition of your book (paperback plus hardcover, paperback plus eBook, etc.) you'll need an ISBN for each. If you buy your own ISBNs from Bowker you are identified as the publisher.
2. Use a self-publishing service like Bookmobile that can provide an ISBN for you. This is usually more cost effective than buying them yourself unless you plan on publishing more than one book. Note that the publishing service will be identified as the publisher of your book.

ISBN DOS AND DON'TS

Do

- Assign a unique ISBN to each edition of your book: paperback, hardcover, eBook, audiobook, revised editions, and so on.

Don't

- Use an ISBN from somebody else's book. It will screw things up for you, and for them, because retailers and others will be totally confused and will have difficulty finding and ordering either book.
- Re-use ISBNs. Same reasons as above.
- Create multiple publishing imprints and randomly use ISBNs registered to one imprint for a book published under another imprint.

BARCODES

The barcode on the back of a book encodes the book's ISBN. It is used at multiple points in the book distribution chain to process books for shipping or sale. The barcode may have the list price for the book encoded as well as the ISBN. A $14.95 book, for example, would have the code 01495 appended to the ISBN. Publishers sometimes choose not to encode the price, but print it elsewhere on the book cover. In that case, the price code is 90000. In any case the list price must be printed on the book cover for distribution to the book trade.

You can purchase barcodes from Bowker or from your book printer. If you are using a self-publishing service they can provide them. The barcode is furnished as an image file that you can place on your book cover in InDesign or Quark. At 100 percent size, a barcode is 2-3/16 x 1 inches. There are rules for how much it can be reduced or enlarged in size, the amount of white space around it, and what color it can be printed in; all designed to keep it readable to machines and humans. See bisg.org/page/BarcodingGuidelines for details.

2. **SRDP PRINTERS,** which use digital printing equipment, are best for print runs of up to 1,000 because your cost per book will almost certainly be lower than offset in this quantity range. SRDP printers offer an almost unlimited degree of customization. They also produce printed proofs for your approval, which enables quality control to a much higher degree than is possible with POD.
3. **OFFSET PRINTERS,** which use traditional offset printing presses, have significantly lower cost per book than either POD or SRDP printers starting at about 1,500 copies. Above 2,000 copies, they are unbeatable. Like SRDP printers, they can offer almost unlimited customization, and they provide printed proofs for your approval, maximizing your control over the final quality of your books.

If you decide to go with a POD printer such as Createspace or Blurb, you'll need to familiarize yourself with their specific online design tools. (Alternatively, for art books, some common photography software programs such as Lightroom offer options for creating books that are then printed by POD printers they're affiliated with.) But again, because these tools—and often the resulting print quality—are so limited, POD isn't recommended; so this chapter doesn't cover those design tools. We feel strongly about this (in case you couldn't tell); but if you're curious, go ahead and check out one or two of these options yourself—because they are aimed at publishing novices, the tools are pretty basic and self-explanatory.

If you plan on printing at an SRDP or offset printer as recommended, you have two options: 1) use professional page layout software like Adobe InDesign or Quark Xpress, or 2) hire a pro who does.

OPTION ONE: PAGE LAYOUT PROGRAMS

Whether you're an old hand with page layout software or you're learning it for the first time, it's helpful to be familiar with the basics of the book printing process in order to understand how the process is impacted by the files you'll create. As with explanations of the different kinds of printers, this process is covered in more detail in chapter 3, but here's the basic process:

1. You design the cover and interior pages of your book in page layout software. You review as many rounds of proofs as it takes to make the book perfect, making corrections before sending the files to the printer, because it becomes much more expensive to make corrections once the printing setup process is begun.
2. You create PDF files of the cover and interior, making sure that all resources are embedded (fonts, images, etc.). Send these files to the book printer you've selected.
3. The printer sends your files through the preflight department in order to find any immediate problems (with fonts, color spaces, etc.). If any issues are discovered they may just fix it, or bounce it back to you if it is a problem that they can't fix for one reason or another.
4. After preflight, the printer runs your files through a Raster Image Processor (RIP, often used by printers as a verb or adjective—i.e., the files are RIPed), which converts images to the halftone dots required for printing in CMYK, and type vectors into smoothly-rendered letterforms.
5. The printer produces proofs of the cover and interior from the RIPed files. These proofs may be a post-RIP PDF, which you can view online, or they may be printed. Offset printers generally use inkjet printers for color proofs. SRDP printers will likely use the actual presses that the book is to be printed on to produce the proofs. Printed proofs are overnighted to you for your review and approval. For a book that includes high-quality images, printed proofs are especially critical.
6. You review the proofs, requesting changes or indicating "OK to print." A critical point: when you say "OK to print," you are saying that you will accept the books regardless of any errors, as long as those errors showed in the proofs you reviewed and approved.
7. After you OK the proofs, the cover and interior pages are printed, assembled into finished books in the bindery, and shipped to wherever you instruct.

The cost of just the paper in a run of books may be thousands of dollars. Add in the cost of digital impressions, the capital cost of very expensive presses and binding gear, and the skilled labor, and a run may cost thousands or tens of thousands. So there is a lot at risk, and nobody wants problems—least of all you and the printer! It's useful to understand what elements of page layout software ensure that this high-stakes process happens smoothly and without costly delays or quality hiccups. Following are some key features of professional page layout software that come into play during this process.

FINE TYPOGRAPHY

Don't underestimate the critical role that fine typography plays in creating a book that doesn't look homemade. Even art books full of beautiful images, where the text is not the main event, are severely diminished by clumsy, slap-dash type design in the boring default typefaces of every business document (Times Roman or Helvetica). But good typography is more than just the choice of typeface. Typography is itself a craft, and the right tools provide the level of control required for that craftsmanship. They need to include ultra-precise control of type sizes, line spacing, character spacing, word spacing, hyphenation, widows and orphans, and more. Also, they provide in-depth access to special characters like old-style figures and ligatures. Page layout programs that fulfill this requirement include Adobe InDesign and Quark Xpress.

SUPPORT FOR IMAGES IN PROFESSIONAL FORMATS

Any professional page layout program must support any kind of image file—black-and-white line art, grayscale, color—in any file format including TIFFs, JPEGs, PDFs, EPSs, and so on. In particular, when printing full color on a professional-grade digital press or an offset press, the software must be able to support the CMYK color space with a high level of control. The vast majority of high-quality color presses use the Cyan-Magenta-Yellow-Black subtractive color space. Digital cameras and scanners, on the other hand, are universally designed around the Red-Green-Blue (RGB) additive color space. Managing the RGB to CMYK conversion is critical to printing high-quality images, and you need software that enables a high degree of control. Again, Adobe InDesign and Quark Xpress stand out here.

A NOTE ABOUT COVER DESIGN

Your printer should provide you with a detailed cover layout template for your book, based on the page count of the book, the text paper selected, and the cover materials selected. (The next chapter, which details the printing process, provides more information about these choices.) This template will show all measurements for the spine, front cover, back cover, and bleed, and includes an allowance in the spine width for the thickness of the cover. For dust jackets, the template will also show flap dimensions and all-important allowances for where the dust jacket wraps around the hinges and foreedges of the case. If you follow these templates accurately, it is the printer's problem—not yours—if a cover or dust jacket doesn't fit. Provide an inaccurate cover layout and it is your problem.

PORTABILITY AND PRINTABILITY

Normally, the files provided to the book printer are PDFs created by the page layout software, one for the cover or dust jacket, and one for the interior pages. While PDF is a standard, all PDFs are not created equal—PDFs created by a nonprofessional with Microsoft Word, for example, are notorious for their ability to choke a RIP and introduce terrible font rendering errors, as well as for offering almost zero control over image rendering. Professional page layout programs have been tested with hundreds of different configurations of RIPs and presses at printing companies printing billions if not trillions of pages a year. Even so, issues sometimes crop up, especially with complex, multiple-layer dust jacket or cover designs. When they do, if you are using an industry-standard page layout program such as InDesign or Quark, the printer will be able to troubleshoot and correct the problem. If you're using software designed for business and personal correspondence such as Word or Pages, you're likely in for a frustrating and expensive bout of detective work to root out and rectify the problem. Once again, there are only two page layout programs that satisfy these requirements: Adobe InDesign and Quark Xpress.

Given the above, it would appear that InDesign or Quark Xpress are your only real options. And once upon a time, Quark Xpress was top dog. It was by the far the best page layout program, it had the best support in commercial print environments, and it had 95% marketshare among pros. But it was an incredibly arrogant company, charging premium prices for upgrades and acting as if customers were a nuisance. For a long time Quark refused to port Xpress to Mac OS X, and tried to push design professionals to the ugly side (Windows). Fred Ebrahimi, the CEO, was notorious for publicly insulting customers, including, at one point, major book publishers. Then Adobe developed a com-

BEWARE THE LURE OF PHOTOSHOP

Many photographers are fluent in Photoshop, and occasionally some of them turn to Photoshop to lay out photo book pages or book covers. While Photoshop is the gold-standard image editing program for professional print applications, it kind of sucks when it comes to creating a book cover or interior pages. From the point of view of the person laying out the book—you—it has poor facilities for managing multiple page documents and controlling typography. From the point of view of a printer using a RIP feeding a CMYK press, it is a quandary: type is bitmapped—negating those features of the RIP that specialize in rendering type properly—unless you specifically tell it to output the type in vector format when you create the PDF. Even then, the PDF is difficult to debug if there are any printing issues, which there are likely to be because the printer needs to do things that you never even notice (such as fine-tuning the spine width of a paperback cover) in order that your book print optimally. Best to avoid all these issues and stick with InDesign.

pletely new page layout package called InDesign. InDesign 1.0 was pretty rudimentary, but it had some really cool features: it ran on OS X, the price was right, and it wasn't produced by the hated Quark organization. And Adobe kept working on it. In only a few years InDesign owned the market. End of story, actually, except that we're kind of back to square one, with Adobe exercising the kind of feudal dominance over the business that Quark once did. The king is dead; long live the king.

So you've probably figured out what the conclusion is: if you are going to lay out your book yourself, and you want to produce professional-level pages and cover design, do yourself a huge favor and use InDesign. It has a fairly steep learning curve (though but no more so than Photoshop, for example) and it has great book-oriented features. Don't even think about anything else. Not Microsoft Word, Photoshop, Latex, or cool open source software. There are, honestly, no alternatives to Adobe InDesign: when you hand off a complicated file to someone who's going to run it on a million-dollar digital press or a five-million-dollar offset press, the files have to work, and every book printer in the world is intimately familiar with printing from InDesign-created files.

OPTION TWO: HIRING A PRO

When a book publisher publishes a book, they use a professional book designer to design the cover and lay out the pages. This is also an option for individuals. While hiring a pro costs more than DIY, the results are more likely to reflect the level of quality that a consumer or collector is going to expect. (The exception to this rule is, of course, if you have the eye and skill set of a pro. But even an average consumer can spot when a book's design is amateurish, and even great artists don't necessarily make great book designers.) Also, an experienced book designer will bring to the project specialist knowledge that can help you get the best printed book for your dollar.

Furthermore, it's a mistake to think that your sibling, nephew, niece, uncle, dachshund, or whoever can do the job because they have a computer and took an art class. And even true professional graphic designers aren't necessarily up to speed on designing books. Graphic designers are specialists: one who knows how to design a book might do lousy product labels, and vice versa. In addition, a specialist book designer will likely have lower fees than, say, a graphic designer who is used to the plump fees paid by ad agencies. Although sometimes the agency designer will lowball their fees because of the glamour of book design, generally they are not bringing book design experience as part of what they offer.

The upshot: if you are not going to do it yourself, what you want is a good *book* designer. That designer should work in either InDesign or Quark Xpress—and in 98 out of 100 cases, it will be the former.

WHERE ARE ALL THE BOOK DESIGNERS?

Book designers either work as freelancers on a book-by-book basis for publishers, work as employees of publishers, or work for companies that provide services to book publishers. Often, a publisher will hire one designer for the cover of the book and another for the interior of the book, because these are specialties in themselves. But that's not always appropriate, whether because of budget concerns or the type of book under consideration. (For a novel, the cover design is like a movie poster—all about drama, conveying an emotion, grabbing attention—while the interior should be well-designed but not particularly obtrusive. Those are two very different design tasks. The purpose of an art book, on the other hand, is to showcase the art: one of the images should be on the front cover, and the design of the cover and interior should be in total harmony. That means one designer.)

Freelance book designers are all around the country, though they tend to cluster in centers of publishing. Try Googling "book designer, [your city]" to find freelancers in your area. Another option is to tap professional associations, whose websites may have freelancer directories. See appendix C for a partial listing of such organizations.

WHAT A BOOK DESIGNER DOES

Professional book designers don't just sit down at the computer and start hacking out pages in InDesign. They start by planning the book, based on the text and images you provide. They will choose, or help you choose, a page size that best fits your project without being uneconomical (a difference of 1/8" in a page dimension can mean thousands of dollars in additional printing costs). They can advise you on paper selection and printing processes. They are usually typeface maniacs and will propose typefaces you have never heard of but that are the right balance between cool and classic. They will do sample designs of the cover and interior—based on your initial input—for you to approve prior to doing final layouts. They will make printed proofs of the cover and all the pages for your review and proofreading. They will make corrections based on your review. (There are always corrections, and multiple rounds of page proofs.) They will prepare the files properly for printing either on digital or offset presses.

STAGES IN WORKING WITH A BOOK DESIGNER

Stage 1: Get a Design Estimate

After you've identified a book designer you're interested in working with, you'll need to give them some basic information in order for them to provide you with an estimate of their design fees. The request for an estimate should include:

- *Title:* Title of your book (or at least a working title).
- *Frontmatter:* Number of frontmatter pages.
- *Text elements:* A list of all other text elements of the book: introduction, preface, chapters, image captions, end notes, and so on, along with word or character counts.
- *Images:* Number of color images in the book and number of black-and-white images in the book, if any.
- *Page layout guidance:* Rough idea of the layout you're imagining. This may be especially important for art or other image-heavy books. For example, if you have 40 images, are they going to be laid out one per page, or will some pages have more than one image? If the images are one-per-page, will the facing pages have captions, or another image? You get the idea.
- *Page size:* Rough idea of the page size you are imagining. A smaller book with a square page? A medium-sized book in a portrait-format page? A landscape-format book with the largest page size you can get without taking out a second mortgage for printing?
- *Binding:* Paperback or hardcover with dust jacket. If you haven't made up your mind, ask for an estimate for a paperback, with the additional cost to design a hardcover broken out. (It takes more time and is trickier to design a dust jacket than a paperback cover.)
- *Timeframe:* When you will have all the original materials ready for the designer and when do you want to go the printer.

The information listed above should be sufficient for the designer to give you a quote. It also demonstrates that you are organized, which is important, because a client who wastes time is an unprofitable client. And while it's safe to say that book designers are in it because they love good design and well-made books, they are also trying to make a living.

Stage 2: Hand Off Your Book Materials to the Designer

Organize your book before handing it off. Make a list of all the text and image elements, in the order they are to appear in the book—this is the plan for the

INVIOLABLE RULES FOR THE BOOK DESIGN PROCESS

Book design has well-established procedures for ensuring that 1) work gets done efficiently, 2) errors have the maximum opportunity to be caught and corrected before going to press, and 3) nobody goes nuts. (Very large books, especially, can completely overwhelm anyone without good organizational skills, causing the project to spiral downward into a chaos of typos, mixed-up image versions, and worse.)

This means that there are rules, and however you might feel about rules in general, beware that *the rules of producing a book cannot be violated without financial and aesthetic risk of the ugliest kind!* Here are the rules.

1. Verbal instructions do not count. Every instruction must be emailed or put on paper and delivered. Even the production of a small book requires organizational skills, and part of being organized is to have a paper trail for everything. Also, if and when—sadly—a finished book turns out to have a major problem, everybody can tell whose fault it is.
2. Every step must be done in order and completed before the next step is taken. If you are editing text or images in the middle of the designer's process of making pages or after they have laid out the book, you weren't ready to hand off the book to the designer in the first place. It's like installing the plumbing in your new house after you put the walls up and paint them. The only exception to this rule is a project so massive that tasks must be performed in parallel. But such a book project requires a dedicated project manager in any case.
3. Each round of proofs should have fewer errors than the previous round. Book design and production is an iterative process: make page proofs, check them for errors (which is not the same as editing them!), fix the errors, make a complete new set of page proofs, check those, correct any errors, make a new set of page proofs. At each step you should only have to check the corrections marked on the previous round of proofs, not recheck every detail that you already checked! And the end of this process, you have pages that are perfect (well, 99.9 percent perfect, in the real world), and files that can be printed.
4. Check your proofs. *Really, really* check them. Then get somebody else to check your proofs. Here's the ultimate reason to check your proofs: after you sign off on them, in writing, you are saying you will accept any errors in the printed books that were on the proofs that you approved.

book that the designer will follow when laying out the pages. List file names both for images and text on the list. Provide printouts of all the text. Put the printouts in order and number the pages, so that if the manuscript is dropped the order can be reconstructed. (These page numbers are temporary—the actual page numbers will be assigned as the pages are laid out.) Provide the text files in Microsoft Word or a compatible format. Provide photographic image files—either from a camera or scanner—in the highest resolution you have, ideally in PSD (Photoshop) format. Image files from illustration programs like Adobe Illustrator should be provided in their native file format. A key point: for color images, unless you want the designer to tweak your images, they should be edited and soft proofed using a CMYK profile on a calibrated monitor. (Consult with your printer on whether they should be left in RGB or converted to CMYK before submission, and see the next section for more information on optimizing image quality for printing.) If you have a rough layout on paper you want to give to the designer, that's great: it doesn't have to be perfectly laid out or even in color.

Stage 3: Page Layout, an Iterative Process

Here's what the back-and-forth with a designer typically looks like, once you've handed off your materials:

1. The designer produces sample designs of the cover (or dust jacket) and interior, showing their type choices, positioning of images, and so on.
2. You approve the sample designs—or not, in which case the designer goes back to the drawing board. (They will likely have a stipulation in their proposal about how many times they are willing to do so.)
3. With approved designs, the designer lays out every page with all type and images in position and produces proofs for you to review. Those proofs may be just black-and-white laser prints. That's okay—they are just to check all the type and the details of the layout.
4. You check the paper proofs, marking any corrections.
5. The designer makes the corrections in the files and produces the next round of page proofs for you to check. The designer will likely charge by the hour for making corrections. If they are pros, they won't charge for any errors they made, but will charge for any changes you make or corrections to errors that were in the original materials you provided.
6. When you check each round of page proofs, you should only have to check the specific things you marked on the previous page proofs. Therefore, the amount of checking diminishes with each round of page proofs. (One of the errors rookie book designers make is to allow things not marked for correction to reflow or move around between page proofs. This means that things that were checked before have to be checked again, a major time-waster that slows down the whole process. Plus, it's scary: what if they hose up the pages before producing the final files for the printer?)
7. When you get the set of page proofs that has everything the way you want it, the designer is done except for providing the PDF files for the printer. As noted above, these are not just PDF files like you might produce out of Word or from Preview on a Mac—they should be set up according to specific instructions provided by the printer.

The cover design process is similar to that of the page proof iterations described above, except that proofs are more likely to be in color with each round.

Stage 4: Send Files to the Printer

You can have the designer send the files to printer you have chosen, or you can do it yourself along with your order. But the designer is not done yet: if things need to be changed or errors corrected after you see the printer's proofs (yes, more proofs to check!), sometimes the designer must make the changes if they are extensive enough that they can't be made in the relatively rigid file structure of the PDFs provided to the printer.

Hiring a professional book designer is not for everybody. Those who have design skills themselves will likely want to take the DIY route. Those who are just printing a handful of books might be better off using tools provided by POD services. But if you have invested a lot of effort in your book, want the best presentation possible, and are investing thousands of dollars in printing hundreds or thousands of copies of your book, a professional book designer can be a critical investment.

FOR ILLUSTRATED BOOKS: OPTIMIZING IMAGE QUALITY FOR PRINTING

Regardless of how you print your book, it can be a challenge to ensure that the images on the printed pages of your books are true to your vision. So whether you work with a designer or handle book design yourself, if your book includes images, they need to be optimized for printing during the design stage.

There are three different categories of printable images: full-color, continuous tone black-and-white, and line art. Different processes govern the printing of different types of images.

PRINTING FULL-COLOR IMAGES

Depending on the image and the type of press being used, color images are printed using one of three processes.

Full-Color Printing

Full-color printing refers to color photographs or artwork. All color commercial presses, whether offset or digital, print using four "process colors": cyan, magenta, yellow and black (CMYK). A full-color image can be "color separated" so that when the four process colors are combined on press they reproduce most—but often not all—of the colors available in the original color image. This color separation can be done in InDesign or by the printer prior to making printing plates for an offset press or sending a print run to a digital color printer.

When printing using process colors, you can also create colors for backgrounds, type elements, and so on by combining the process colors in different percentages. For example, a bright red can be created by setting the color of an object in InDesign to the following levels of process colors:

Cyan: 0%
Magenta: 92%
Yellow: 6%
Black: 0%

Spot-Color Printing

In printing parlance, using a "spot color" means mixing ink to a specific color to use on press. The system used to specify the colors and mix the inks is the Pantone standard. The red color created by mixing process colors described above is approximately matched by an ink color called Pantone 185. Not all Pantone colors can be matched by mixing process colors: The Pantone "gamut," or range of possible colors, is larger than the CMYK gamut. Pantone colors are available when using the offset printing process, and almost never when printing digitally. Generally, it is more expensive to print using spot, or Pantone, colors because the ink has to be custom mixed and the press specially set up and then cleaned up.

One-Color Printing

Most printing done is only one color: black. So, many presses only print one color. On digital one-color presses the color is always black; on an offset press the one color can be any Pantone color.

PRINTING CONTINUOUS TONE BLACK-AND-WHITE IMAGES

All printing is done with solid colors: ink is either on a particular part of the page or it's not. In order to reproduce black-and-white images that have a range of tonal density—paintings, photographs, and so on—the eye is faked out by converting the image into tiny dots, called halftone dots, which can be as fine as 300 to the inch. The size of the dot determines how dark the ink appears on a particular area of the page. A pattern of 90 percent black dots, for example, covers 90 percent of that area of the page with black ink, therefore appearing as a very dark gray. An area made up of 10 percent black dots, on the other hand, appears as a light gray. Color images are created making halftone dot images in each of the process colors.

PRINTING LINE ART IMAGES

Line art images are simply images where halftone screening is not required to reproduce the original art. Type is one example of line art. A pen-and-ink drawing is an example of art that can often be reproduced simply by printing the image as-is without making a halftone screen. However, if an ink drawing had areas of gray or graduated ink washes, it would need to be reproduced by using the halftone process.

When you place a line art image in a page layout program such as InDesign, that image will print black unless you specify otherwise. If cost is no object, you can print line art in any Pantone color on an offset press by setting the color of the image in your page layout file and telling the printer that you want to print the book in black plus a second color. It costs more, because the printer has to make separate plates and run the second color as either an additional pass on a one-color press or as a custom color on a multicolor press. If the book is printing on a CMYK press, the Pantone color will be converted to the closest possible CMYK match, which may or may not be close: there are some Pantone colors that are not reproducible using CMYK. Of course, if the book is printing on a CMYK press, you can also set the color of line art using the CMYK system, which will have more predictable results.

You can also print line art in color on a four-color digital press. Again, set the color of the image in your page layout program, using either CMYK colors or Pantone colors. Because of the fact that all commercial digital presses that print in color use the CMYK color system and do not print Pantone colors, the line art will not print in a solid color but will be made into a four-color halftone via the normal CMYK process, with resultant loss of crispness and potential jaggies along curves (see below for more information). If you set the color of the image using the Pantone system, it will be converted to the closest possible CMYK match for that color.

Because these different types of images use different printing processes, they need to be optimized for printing in different ways. Read on for how to prepare each kind.

PREPARING FULL-COLOR IMAGES

When you are printing photographs in a darkroom or on an inkjet printer, you have the luxury of simply making test prints and tweaking the exposure, contrast, and so on through succeeding tests until you arrive at a print with the qualities you want. True, adopting color management practices like monitor calibration and using color profiles can streamline this process, but they are not strictly necessary. When you go to a photo book printing service, however, unless you have unlimited patience and an unlimited budget, it is not really practical to rely on repeated test prints to maximize the final print quality. Because of this, adopting good color management techniques is your best option for reducing frustration, saving you money, and improving your finished books. And it is not that hard!

Here are the main steps:

- Calibrate your monitor and use a color profile to previsualize—"soft proof"—how your images will print.
- Make sure that all PDF settings are correct when preparing the cover and interior PDFs to send to the printer.
- If you use an SRDP or offset printer, review printed proofs and make changes intelligently.

Because each of these steps takes some time to describe, and this process doesn't apply to everyone, we've put the detailed instructions in appendix D.

PREPARING CONTINUOUS TONE IMAGES

Continuous tone black-and-white images include black-and-white photographs, as well as artwork that has been photographed in black-and-white, such as paintings or lithographs. A black-and-white photograph can have an infinite range of tones, from solid black, through the grays, to the brightest white, though not all images contain the entire range. The halftone process converts that range of grays into an image of solid black ink dots of varying sizes so that it can be printed on a printing press that only has one color of ink. When printed and viewed at normal reading distance, the dots appear to the eye as that range of grays.

In the darkest areas of the photo, the dots will be so big they run together; here the image looks like white dots of varying sizes on a black background. In the lightest areas of the photo, the halftone consists of tiny black dots in a field of white—or more accurately, in a field of whatever color the paper is. In the middle-gray areas of the photo, the area of white and the area of black is 50% black and 50% white.

Formerly, a halftone image was created by taking a picture of the original photograph in a giant camera called a process camera. The halftone dots were created by placing a finely engraved transparent screen directly over the film in the process camera. This special screen resolved the different intensities of light in the image that the process camera's lens focused on the film into dots of varying sizes. Now the dots are formed by software, and imaged via laser or LED directly onto an offset printing plate or onto the imaging drum of a digital press.

Halftone Quality

Theoretically, the best image reproduction quality is obtained when perfect halftone dots are reproduced perfectly on the paper. In reality, the dots are never created or reproduced perfectly. The dots created by the software may not be perfect to begin. Imaging the dots on an offset plate or digital imaging drum involves some further degradation—though much less than in the days of all-film processes! Offset web (roll-fed) presses have some slippage of the fast-moving ribbon of paper as it moves through the press, deforming the dots on the paper. Finally, when a liquid or semi-liquid dot of ink is pressed onto paper it spreads out, both by physical smushing and by seepage out through the fibers of the paper.

The spreading out of halftone dots is called dot gain, and and it is the primary factor that has to be taken into account when creating a halftone. For best quality, a halftone shouldn't be created with a one-to-one mapping from grayscale density to dot density, but such that it will look right after dot gain has occurred on press. In general, this means decreasing the size of the halftone dots in different tonal areas of the image.

Dot gain depends on the quality of the paper and the precision of the press. Coarse, cheap paper like newsprint produces huge dot gain, while fine coated paper will have minimal dot gain. High-speed newspaper presses where the paper is fed through on a roll produce the lowest quality dot. Offset presses that feed the paper in sheets have better registration, or positioning, of the paper as it is printed, resulting in better-formed dots. A similar dynamic applies with digital presses: sheet-feeding allows better print quality than roll-feeding.

Dot Densities for Offset Printing

In a halftone, the darkness of an image is expressed as the percentage of the paper in a given area that is covered by ink: 100 percent is solid ink, 50 percent is half ink and half background paper, 0 percent is no ink. On a cheap newsprint a 50 percent halftone dot may turn into a 70 percent dot as a result of dot gain, drastically darkening the image and eliminating detail from the image. An 80 percent dot will approach 100 percent on cheap newsprint. The trick is to create dots of such a size that when they are printed on a particular press, they undergo dot gain to just the right density. So for a newspaper photo, the image might be adjusted so that the darkest area of the image has 80 percent density.

HALFTONE LINE SCREENS

Halftone dots are usually arranged in a grid, with precise spacing between the centers of the dots. That spacing is called screen ruling, and in North America it is denoted by lines per inch, or lpi. This not the same thing as dots per inch, or dpi, which is used to designate computer screen resolutions and the imaging resolution of a press.

Confusing, yes? Let's clarify with examples from Bookmobile:

Our Océ 6320 monochrome (black-only) digital presses create page images with a resolution of 600 x 1200 dpi. That means that everything on the page is made up of tiny imaging dots that are 1/600" x 1/1200" in size, including type, images, rules, tints, and so on. We run halftones on these presses at 125 lpi, so the spacing between the centers of each of the dots on a halftone is 1/125". Each halftone dot is formed by combining multiple imaging dots.

Our Xerox Color 1000i and 800i presses create page images with a resolution of 2400 x 2400 dpi, so everything on the page is created with tiny dots that are 1/2400" x 1/2400" in size. These presses print halftones at up to 200 lpi, comparable to high quality offset presses.

In theory, using very fine line screens should result in better image detail. However, because of the drastic variability in the ability of a particular combination of press and paper to produce a high-quality halftone dot, finer screen ruling is not necessarily a better screen ruling. To use the extreme example, a 300 lpi printed on a web offset press on newsprint creates an image with all the clarity of a mud puddle, because the dots cannot be resolved. I used to shoot film halftones for newspapers. The editors always pushed for a 120 lpi screen thinking it would improve photo reproduction, but in reality the best images—crisp, with a good range of tones—were produced using a much lower 85 lpi screen.

Here are typical halftone screen values:

- Web offset, uncoated paper: 120 lpi
- Sheetfed offset, uncoated paper: 133 lpi
- Sheetfed offset, coated paper: 200 lpi
- Monochrome digital press (toner-based): 125 lpi
- Four-color digital press (toner-based): 200 lpi

Continuous inkjet press manufacturers claim up to 175 lpi, but based on the samples I've seen, that's pushing it. Check with the printing company actually operating the press.

At the other end of the tonal range, the lightest highlight areas, it looks weird to have the edge of image exactly the same density as the background paper. In fact, it looks like a mistake. Best practice is to create enough dot in the highlights so that there is a visible edge to the photograph. Depending on the press and paper, this could be 4 to 10 percent—higher quality presses on coated paper can reproduce a clean 4 percent dot, which would disappear on newsprint printed on a web press. The optimum densities for printing on newsprint will be something like 80 percent maximum dot, 10 percent minimum dot. Printing on a sheetfed press on coated stock it will be something like 97 percent maximum dot, 2 percent minimum dot, and on a web press 95 percent/ 3 percent.

You should ask your printer what the minimum and maximum dot densities are appropriate for your particular book. They'll take into account the paper and the press when giving you an answer. See "Adjusting Dot Densities in Grayscale Images" in this chapter for a step-by-step of how to make the necessary changes in Photoshop.

Dot Densities for Digital Printing

Digital presses print either using toner (dry pigmented powder) or liquid ink jets. Toner and inkjet presses have very different dot gain characteristics.

TONER-BASED DIGITAL PRINTING. There is no need to compensate for dot gain on these presses. This is because 1) the toner is dry when applied to the paper and does not bleed out into the fibers and 2) the presses have closed-loop image quality monitoring so that the sheets coming off the press are constantly monitored and the press adjusted to maintain accurate densities.

INKJET DIGITAL PRINTING. There are two kinds of inkjet presses:

- *Drop-on-demand inkjet presses* deliver precisely metered drops of ink to precise positions on the page. They can produce extremely high quality images, but because of their very slow speed they are rarely used to print books.
- *Continuous inkjet presses* work by modulating thousands of continuous streams of ink coming from microscopic nozzles as the paper whips by underneath. The fastest continous inkjet presses feed paper at 1,000 feet per minute! Continuous inkjet presses are relatively new to the book printing market, but they are becoming a viable replacement for offset and toner-based digital for applications where high quality is not a requirement, such as textbooks. Continuous inkjet presses cannot currently come close to toner-based digital or offset presses in terms of quality, but they can provide an economical alternative at some run lengths for low quality work.

As with offset printing, ask the printer for guidelines on setting grayscale densities so you can optimize the images for a continuous inkjet press. And again, see "Adjusting Dot Densities in Grayscale Images" in this chapter for a step-by-step of how to make the necessary changes in Photoshop.

Adjusting Dot Densities in Grayscale Images

Here's a simple—actually, oversimplified—way to adjust the minimum and maximum densities in an image in Photoshop:

Convert the image to grayscale. Use the curves tool or the levels tool to set maximum and minimum densities of the image to the percentages recommended by your printer. Let's say that your printer recommends a maximum 97 percent and minimum 3 percent density. Using the curves tool, you can just grab the endpoint of the standard curve and move them so that an input of 100 percent has an output of 97 percent. Then grab the other end of the line and move it so that an input of 0 percent results in an output of 3 percent.

This method works, but individual images may require more extensive manipulation to print optimally. Some images, frankly, will never print well on commercial printing equipment because all the detail is in highlight or deep shadow areas where it is very difficult for presses to print distinct gradations. Often, there is a lot of detail in midtones that is easy to see on screen, and very difficult to actually print. For most images, this might not even matter. If you are doing a fine art photo or art book, printed proofs from the printer are an invaluable way to see the results of your tweaking, and make further adjustments as necessary.

Ask Your Printer for Guidelines

Just to reiterate: Whatever kind of press your book will be printed on, ask your printer for guidelines for preparing grayscale images. They should have complete information available for you, and you can adjust your images accordingly.

PREPARING LINE ART

As we noted earlier, in printing nomenclature, line art is an image in which the original consists only of solid color against a white background. Examples of line art include type, pen-and-ink drawings, and prints from wood engravings. Remember that images with any kind of gradation of tones in color or black-and-white—watercolors, oil paintings, stone lithographs, and, of course, photographs—are not line art and must be converted to a halftone image in order to print on a press. (See previous section for details on this process.)

Line art is usually simple to prepare for printing: scan the image as "black-and-white" instead of as grayscale, sizing it to close to the final printing size as you scan. (Different scanning software uses different terminology for the line art setting: "black-and-white" and "type" are two common terms.) Scan at 600 dpi (dots per inch): 300 dpi is actually not fine enough to preserve fine line art detail.

If you are reproducing a line art image with a digital camera, you'll have to manipulate the image in Photoshop, Pixelmator, or another image editing package to convert it to grayscale from RGB, bring the background tone down to 0 percent, and set the darkest tones appropriately.

If the line art image is created with type fonts, no conversions should be necessary: save the image as a PDF and place it. The same is true for images created with vector image editing software such as Adobe Illustrator.

While usually simple to do, there are a few pitfalls in handling line art images:

- Reducing the size of the image too much when it is placed in the page layout program can result in making lines too fine to print.
- Enlarging the image too much when it is placed in the page layout program can result in scan-line jaggies showing along curves. Remember that if you scale up a 600 dpi image in the page layout program to 200 percent of the original size, the effective resolution is 300 dpi (600 dpi / 200% = 300 dpi).
- Some artwork that is classified as line art, such as pen-and-ink drawings, can actually have subtle gradations of tone. If those gradations are eliminated by converting the image to pure black-and-white, the quality of the image may be degraded in comparison to the original. If you scan such an image and find that prints from the image look somehow lacking, the loss of subtle gradations could be the culprit. In such cases, it may pay to scan the image as a halftone, convert it to grayscale, use the Photoshop curves or levels tool to set the background grayscale value to 0 percent to eliminate the background tone, and set the darkest part off the image to 97 percent. There is a tradeoff here: because halftone screen rulings (lpi, or lines per inch) are coarser than image dots (dpi, dots per inch), the resulting jaggies in curves of the halftoned image may be more objectionable than the loss of subtle gradations from just scanning the image as line art. Test prints are definitely in order here if optimum quality is desired.

Speaking of test prints: use an office laser printer to get an initial idea of how a line art will print. You'll see any gross quality problems. However, such a test print will not print exactly as an offset or digital press does. The proofs an offset printer provides will give a better idea of the ultimate printing quality, though usually still not exact. If you use a digital book printer, you should get proofs printed on the actual press the book will print on, which is the most accurate kind of proof.

CHAPTER 3

PLANNING AND EXECUTING YOUR CAMPAIGN

Now that you've designed your book and created your budget, you're ready to plan and launch your campaign. Kickstarter (https://www.kickstarter.com/) is far and away the most popular crowdfunding platform for creative work: they claim over 162,000 successful projects, backed by 16 million people, with over $4 billion pledged. They have a designated publishing category, which is one of their largest and most active. Publishing projects are also funded in the Comics and Photography categories, and some projects in the Games category include books.

Indiegogo (https://www.indiegogo.com/) is another popular option, though it's got a broader focus than just creative projects, and their fee structure is somewhat different. There are also smaller niche crowdfunding platforms aimed specifically at publishing, such as Publishizer (https://publishizer.com/), which queries publishers on behalf of successful creators, and the newly minted PubLaunch (https://www.publaunch.com/, currently only available in beta), which will offer a way for creators to with people from various publishing services as they plan their campaigns. Yet other sites use different models, such as Unbound (https://unbound.com/), which acts as a publisher itself for writers who have pitched ideas on their site that have garnered enough support. See appendix E for a partial listing of crowdfunding sites that support publishing projects.

Depending on your project, it may be worth investigating these and other options, but because Kickstarter is by far the most tried-and-true platform, as well as the one that receives the most traffic and has launched the most successful publishing projects, our focus is on their model. (It's worth noting that using another model might entail significant differences from the process we lay out in this book. For instance, a budget that takes into account pre-sales, as would be the case for a project using Authr, would look very different from the sample budget we set out in chapter 1 using the Kickstarter model.)

Kickstarter provides a lot of information on running a successful campaign, and their website is probably the best resource for comprehensive information about designing your campaign. Their Creator Handbook offers specific advice on everything from designing your project page to promoting your campaign to communicating with backers.

But there's also no substitute for learning from experience. So we've tapped a few successful Kickstarter creators to ask them about the campaigns they designed for their publishing projects—especially what they learned along the way and what they might do differently in hindsight. The following case studies look at three successful publishing projects: a book of travel writing and photography, a graphic novel, and a literary journal. We asked the creators some questions to find out how they mounted their successful campaigns and what advice they have about the process.

TAKK: EXPLORATIONS OF NORDIC CAFÉ CULTURE

TAKK: Explorations of Nordic Café Culture (https:takktravels.blogspot.com) is a book of writing and travel photography focusing on Scandinavian coffee shop culture. The book is striking: in addition to beautifully designed interior pages with lovely photographs, the simple embossed cover makes it an enticing physical artifact. The *TAKK* creators Samantha Albert and Corey Kingston used Kickstarter to raise over $16,000 for their 3-month trip through Denmark, Iceland, Sweden, and Finland to research the book, as well as for the costs of producing and distributing the book. Sam and Corey said of their experience:

"Running a successful Kickstarter campaign really is a full-time job, and asking your friends and family for money is not that fun. Be prepared to swallow your pride in order to complete your funding goals. Get creative with how you solicit donations. Have fun with your Kickstarter campaign and make sure your aesthetic and copy is in line with your personality and project."

Here's more from Corey.

DESCRIBE THE GENESIS OF YOUR PROJECT. DID YOU HAVE ANY PREVIOUS PUBLISHING EXPERIENCE? WHY DID YOU DECIDE THAT KICKSTARTER WAS THE WAY TO GO?

TAKK: Explorations of Nordic Café Culture was conceived by Sam while she was doing research for a café she wanted to open in Seattle. At the time, I was studying in Copenhagen and was very sad to leave the city. When Sam approached me to be the photographer for the book, I jumped at the chance. Neither of us had experience in publishing, and that may have served us, because our naiveté pushed us to step up to the challenge. We decided to do a Kickstarter campaign because we didn't have a book deal and we needed to generate money for our research, travels, equipment, post production, and printing. I had done a Kickstarter campaign before while working at an architecture firm, so I was familiar with the process and knew that it could be successful if we put the time and energy into it.

WHAT WERE THE MOST IMPORTANT CONSIDERATIONS IN DESIGNING YOUR KICKSTARTER CAMPAIGN? WHAT STEPS DID YOU TAKE IN PLANNING IT?

We spent a lot of time ensuring the video and graphics of the project were interesting and spoke to our aesthetic, which we were already starting to form at that point. We put a lot of energy into the copy of the Kickstarter, making sure that the project and our mission were easy to comprehend. We tried to make it clear how we were planning to achieve our goals and what the contributions would be used for.

WHAT DID YOU DO TO GET THE WORD OUT ABOUT YOUR KICKSTARTER?

We both worked incredibly hard at marketing the project—that was the most time-consuming part. Not only did we send the Kickstarter link out to all of our personal contacts, we sent it to all of the organizations that we thought would be interested in donating, including Nordic clubs across the world, schools, consulates, Nordic ambassadors etc., and we were constantly promoting our Kickstarter on social media.

WHAT STUMBLING BLOCKS DID YOU RUN INTO ALONG THE WAY? WHAT DID YOU LEARN AS YOU WENT?

Oh man, we hit so many blocks along the way and learned so much. Pretty much the whole project was us stumbling into a problem and then finding a way to work around that problem. Whether this was in our Kickstarter, the travel research, or the post production of writing and assembling the book. Then the printing/self-publishing process was a whole other animal that we had to figure out, as well as distribution and sales. Without our initial naiveté and commitment to writing the book, I don't think we would have completed *Takk*. Making *Takk* was a huge learning experience that was frustrating at times, but also incredibly rewarding.

WHAT ADVICE DO YOU HAVE FOR SOMEONE WHO IS UNDERTAKING A KICKSTARTER PUBLISHING PROJECT?

I would suggest that the person undertaking a Kickstarter publishing project take the time to really figure out the needs of the project and the time it will realistically take so that one can plan for it financially, professionally, and personally. The more detailed one can be, the better. Each detail, like sending out the rewards for a ten-dollar donation, for example, can take a lot of time. The more information you have about how you will complete your project at the Kickstarter stage, the more successful you will be.

WEBB: THE BIG RACE

Created by Mike Cucka, John Salimbene, and Brad Gorby, Webb: The Big Race (https://www.facebook.com/webbgraphicnovel) is the story a stock car racer (named Webb) fighting the forces of consumerism run amok. In Webb's world, people get turned into actual product mascots and have their lives subsumed by marketing campaigns. But Webb wants none of it.

The three creators raised over $8,000 on Kickstarter to bring their graphic novel to life. Their campaign included some unique elements—for example, one of the awards offered to backers was to be added to the book as a product mascot. Once funded, they spent the rest of the year writing and illustrating the book. Backers were updated on their trip to Comic Con, where they introduced the character of Webb, along with preliminary sketches, and of course the news when books were shipped out.

Here's what Mike had to say about their campaign.

DESCRIBE THE GENESIS OF YOUR PROJECT. WHY DID YOU DECIDE THAT KICKSTARTER WAS THE WAY TO GO IN PUBLISHING IT?

Our graphic novel, *Webb*, was born of lunchtime conversations we [Mike and John] had in the early 1990s while working in corporate America. Inspired by Wacky Packages, Saturday morning cartoons, advertising mascots and the like, we just had fun coming up with imaginary products that made us laugh over our triangular corporate sandwiches served in too-long, tedious corporate meetings.

We eventually turned these products into product mascots and created a world of characters around them. Then, in our first foray into writing, we conceived of the story as a graphic novel. That was a challenge as neither of us had ever written a graphic novel before and neither of us could illustrate. We needed to find an artist (that's another long story!).

MAAEMO

Oslo, Norway

At Maaemo, a groundbreaking two-Michelin-star restaurant in Oslo, coffee is presented—without cream or sugar—as the final course of the culinary experience. Here, the traditional Norwegian steeping method of *kokekaffe* is used to prepare the coffee.

Kokekaffe is the oldest way to make coffee in Norway. It simply entails throwing some ground coffee into a pot of boiling water, and voilà—the coffee is "cooked." Many Norwegian hikers still make coffee this way while on the trail. Maaemo's sommelier, Pontus Dahlstrøm, told us, over a discussion of their favorite coffee memories, how the team at Maaemo realized their best coffee moments were "out hiking with the guys, and making kokekaffe around a campfire." This sparked the inspiration for the coffee at Maaemo.

Here, kokekaffe is prepared to perfection. Pontus first weighs the coffee beans to the ounce before grinding them to the perfect particle size. He then submerges the grounds into boiling water for precisely four minutes, thereby yielding the truest flavor of the bean. He presents the coffee in a beautiful copper kettle set atop a kerosene flame, which is suspended over a bed of moss no less, before pouring the perfect cup. Not only is this coffee full of flavor, but also it's full of history, triggering warm memories from the trail.

Takk: Explorations of Nordic Café Culture, travel writing and photography project by Samantha Albert and Corey Kingston.

Webb, comic project by Mike Cucka, John Salimbene, and Brad Gorby.

Moss, writing anthology project by Connor Guy and Alex Davis-Lawrence.

Back then, with no social media resources available (and, of course, no crowd sourced funding other than asking relatives and close friends to donate to our cause), we were limited in our ability to gather enough resources to move the project along to completion.

Fast forward to 2014. We realized Kickstarter could be a great way to not only gather resources to finalize our project but also help spread the word. A side benefit, was that we had to be able to present our idea in a concise, clear and compelling way. Getting the premise down can be a real struggle for any creator and it sure was for us.

WHAT WERE THE MOST IMPORTANT CONSIDERATIONS IN DESIGNING YOUR KICKSTARTER CAMPAIGN? WHAT STEPS DID YOU TAKE IN PLANNING IT?

Video (did we want one?) and reward design (what could we offer?) were key considerations. To figure all that out, we looked at a variety of blogs and such detailing success factors for Kickstarter projects. It was also helpful to review the top ten or so successful Kickstarter projects at the time (both of our type and overall) to see how they put their stories together: project name, video content and construction, project description, reward levels, creator bios, etc.

As we were writing a graphic novel, we were fortunate to have a lot of artwork lying around. This was great material to use with a voiceover on a video. We taught ourselves iMovie and put a video together and then wrote the project description to complement that.

HOW DID YOU EXECUTE THAT PLAN? WHAT DID YOU DO TO GET THE WORD OUT ABOUT YOUR KICKSTARTER?

We used Basecamp to share content with our team (three of us in various locations across the United States). That allowed us easy and quick review of copy, video, etc. and management of the overall process.

We had created a Facebook page for our project about a year before launching the Kickstarter. Primarily, we used that Facebook page and Kickstarter's platform to get the word out. We also emailed friends, attended local comic book conventions (useful to get mailing list of potential project supporters), created promo items, and did some limited advertising on LinkedIn.

WHAT STUMBLING BLOCKS DID YOU RUN INTO ALONG THE WAY? WHAT DID YOU LEARN AS YOU WENT?

First, I'd say that while our Kickstarter was successful, there is much we'd do differently had we but known what we know now! A few stumbling blocks:

PROJECT DESCRIPTION: Get the story premise concise, clear and compelling. It really has to come to life on the page. If it has a simple and unique idea behind it, your job will be much easier.

VIDEO: It's important to get this right. Show the creators. Bring the story to life, as opposed to talking too much about how the idea came to be and other internally-focused details.

GETTING THE WORD OUT: We would do much more of this and consider more targeted advertising though, of course, one has to consider ROI on that. There's also no substitute for face-to-face contact, so if you're considering a graphic novel, getting exposure at a local show (one of the big shows even better) at the very least gets you contact with a few potential supporters and, perhaps as important, some photographs of fans at your booth that you can share and add to your Kickstarter description to show that there is interest and you are out in the market and believe in what you are doing.

PRODUCT: As the Kickstarter funds were to be used to pay our artist and some of the print costs, we did not have a finished product at the time of the Kickstarter (or the comic book shows we attended). It's great if you can give a sense of what that finished product will look like, to make it easy for the donor to imagine it in their hands. We created an ashcan (promo copy) using artwork we did have on hand.

MANAGEMENT: Don't be afraid to make changes to the Kickstarter content. We didn't do this enough at the start of our project and probably should have. If you get feedback something is not clear or could be better, evaluate its source, gather evidence pro or con and then decide to make a change or not. Kickstarter makes the project description easy to edit and change out images, etc.

REWARDS: It took a little while to figure out rewards based on the most common reward levels we noticed when doing our analysis—it turned out to be tricky for our type of project. You want to give something of value to donors at the higher dollar amounts. For a graphic novel, that meant illustrations or promo items or the ability to "look in" on our conversations as we developed the story. Because we were not the artists, we had to pay to create some of this content. So: Figure out the costs associated with your rewards as well as with your finished product. Add those together. Then decide what you can offer that's valuable but also lets you finish your project.

WHAT OTHER ADVICE DO YOU HAVE FOR SOMEONE WHO IS UNDERTAKING A KICKSTARTER PUBLISHING PROJECT?

Take a look at the projects the Kickstarter team seems to like. See what those projects do well. You may have a project that is simply not likely to be voted a "Favorite Project" but if you can get that exposure, it could help.

Try talking to friends and family first. Kickstarter does take a percentage of your funds raised so if you can get the money you need direct from the source, that will be to your advantage. On the other hand, posting your project to Kickstarter gets you the exposure I mentioned earlier.

Pick a reasonable financial target. You only get the funds if you achieve your goal so don't set your goal too high. Also, you'll probably see more activity early on (when your project shows up as new) and as the deadline of your project approaches and folks might be looking to help pojects that are close to their goals "get over the line."

Also, don't forget to consider printing and fulfillment: The folks at Bookmobile [who handled our printing and fulfillment] were very helpful to us as we got to the product planning and cost estimation stage. As above, know what the costs will be. That also allows you to give an accurate description in the Kickstarter project description (e.g. will it be hardcover or softcover, color or black and white). The last thing you want is to promise full color and then, only after the Kickstarter is complete, realize that while your fundraising goal wasn't actually high enough to deliver on that promise. For fulfillment of rewards, visit the Post Office or UPS and nail down how much it will be to mail out rewards. If you open your Kickstarter up to international audiences, be sure to estimate that postage—which for our 60-page hardcover exceeded $70 in some cases.

MOSS: VOLUME ONE

Moss: Volume One (https://www.mosslit.com/) is an anthology of Northwest writing with a community-first mission and a focus on emerging writers. Started as an online publication by Connor Guy and Alex Davis-Lawrence in 2014, *Moss* ran a Kickstarter campaign in order to launch the first print issue of the journal, which is an anthology of the first three online issues. The campaign successfully raised $4,160—nearly double their goal. Their campaign featured a great video, and the journal they printed delivers on the campaign promise—excellent writing from Northwest authors in a "beautiful, accessible, and tangible print book."

After printing the first issue, Connor and Alex wanted to switch to a subscription model to avoid running a Kickstarter campaign for each print issue.

They now run their subscription service through Patreon (https://www.patreon.com/), another crowdfunding service where backers make recurring (instead of one-time) contributions. Alex says that though the transition wasn't seamless, they've printed a second volume and they're in a great position financially heading into the third volume: "It's made me feel hugely optimistic about *Moss*'s long-term survival."

Here's more from Alex.

DESCRIBE THE GENESIS OF YOUR PROJECT. WHY DID YOU DECIDE THAT KICKSTARTER WAS THE WAY TO GO IN MAKING THE MOVE TO PRINT?

We'd had Moss as an online-only journal for about a year before we decided to make the move to print, but realized that the cost to print even a small run was beyond what we were able to personally fund. Kickstarter was a great fit for a lot of reasons. For one, it's a platform that people in the arts and literary community are immediately familiar with—people trust it, many people already have accounts or have donated to other projects before, and it's clear to people what type of help we're asking for. Second, it offered a lot of key features that were important to us—multiple donation tiers, rich video and photo options, clear fee and payment structures, good built-in messaging and sharing options. Finally, and maybe most importantly, we felt that it was a platform that would let us raise a real amount of money while maintaining our sense of creative integrity—we didn't have to pitch ourselves to anyone other than our actual readers.

WHAT WERE THE MOST IMPORTANT CONSIDERATIONS IN DESIGNING YOUR KICKSTARTER CAMPAIGN? WHAT STEPS DID YOU TAKE IN PLANNING IT?

In terms of planning, I think the biggest practical concerns were finding the right price point for everything and scheduling the campaign effectively. Before we even registered with Kickstarter, we had to price out the cost of printing and shipping the book itself, as well as the other rewards (shirts, totes, stickers, photo prints, and a couple of other things), make sure our goal number accounted for all these costs and for possibly variance in donor levels (for example, we needed to be sure our numbers added up whether we had 100 donors who only bought books or 25 donors who all bought books, shirts, and totes), and make sure that the price point for everything felt reasonable and fair both to our needs and to our audience. (Kickstarter also provides some useful information and statistics on how to price your reward tiers effectively.) And, we wanted to make sure the key dates (the start, the end, delivery dates) would be attainable, and fell on the donation-friendly dates and times—ending a campaign at 2 a.m. on a Sunday night, for example, would make it harder to reach an audience in the critical final hours than if we ended the campaign at 8 p.m. on a Thursday.

WHAT DID YOU DO TO GET THE WORD OUT ABOUT YOUR KICKSTARTER?

Fortunately, we went into the project with a relatively large audience, grown during the first online-only year of issues. We had a mailing list, social media presence, and good relationships with people in the community. We also put together a reading/party to act as a launch event for the Kickstarter. That gave us a big boost in spreading the word, and a strong base of initial donations. We kept the energy up throughout with social posts, personal emails and networking, newsletters to the mailing list, posts on blogs and in the press, and the like.

WHAT STUMBLING BLOCKS DID YOU RUN INTO ALONG THE WAY? WHAT DID YOU LEARN AS YOU WENT?

I had run a successful Kickstarter before (for a short film), so I didn't encounter anything too unexpected with the Moss Kickstarter. I will say that a big lesson I took from the first Kickstarter is to be aware of and prepared for the natural ebb and flow of donations. People tend to donate a lot at the beginning, and a lot at the end—the middle holds a lot of uncertainty. There are always dead periods during a campaign, and you have to have a lot of options and ideas in place to keep the energy up and rebuild the messages around different goals (the ask on day 1 should have a different tone than the ask on day 30, that is to say).

WHAT ADVICE DO YOU HAVE FOR SOMEONE WHO IS UNDERTAKING A KICKSTARTER PUBLISHING PROJECT?

Account for more shipping costs than you expect! In every campaign I've run, pricing shipping effectively has been one of the biggest challenges. Make sure you're accounting for buying the envelopes or mailers, and for specialty shipping cases—international shipping, for example, is extremely expensive compared to domestic shipping—even an unexpected difference of an ounce or two can have a substantial difference in shipping cost, if it bumps you into a higher tier or payment class. Mistakes will probably be made, so leave some cushion for it in your budget. Most of all, remember that USPS Media Mail (by far the cheapest option for mailing books) will be your best friend.

Running a Kickstarter is a lot of work—if you look at the sheer amount of time that goes into setting up and executing a campaign, the reality is that in most cases you'd probably get a better hourly return working at a fast food counter. However, the intangible rewards—the community you build, the sense of ownership your audience feels, the sense of accomplishment you'll feel—are well worth it.

SELECTED BOOK PRINTING EMBELLISHMENTS

For more great book creations see www.bookmobile.com/gallery/.

FRENCH FLAPS ON PAPERBACK

FOIL STAMP

RAIN
of the
FUTURE
Poems by Valerie Mejer
Edited by C.D. Wright

PARTIAL DUSTJACKET

PAPERBACK WITH INSIDE COVER PRINTED, PLUS ENDPAPERS

GATEFOLD

The
Peter Pauper Press
of Peter and Edna Beilenson

PRINTED ENDSHEETS

MULTIPLE HITS FOIL STAMPING

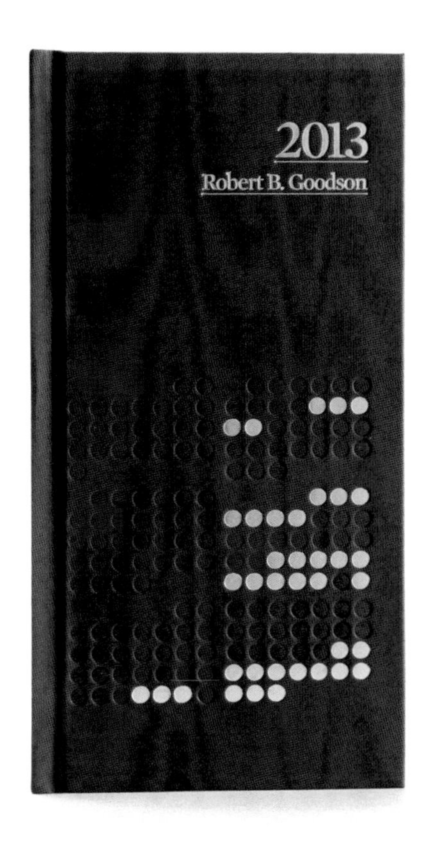

BLIND DEBOSSING

CHAPTER 4

PRINTING YOUR BOOK

In addition to being an efficient and economical way to mass reproduce a book, printing adds value. The printed book is durable, portable, compact, and provides a host of other benefits compared to reading a loose stack of manuscript pages, a Word file, or even an eBook. But it's not inevitable that printing a book adds value. In fact, making the wrong printing choices can subtract value relative to other books in the marketplace. The right printing choices add value by making the book an attractive—if not positively beautiful—object, and optimizing the reading experience.

Here is a partial list of the kinds of value that are affected by choices made when printing a book:

- *Permanence:* Will the book last hundreds of years or self-destruct in two?
- *Legibility:* Is the transmission of information from the page to the reader's eyes clear and direct, or impeded by paper and binding characteristics?
- *Beauty:* Is the book designed to be not only a functional medium, but also a beautiful object?
- *Economy:* Is the money invested in printing the book spent on things that matter to the reader or fripperies that put the unlocking of value at risk?
- *Fidelity:* Is type reproduced cleanly on the page? If there are images, are they reproduced at a quality congruent with their purpose?
- *Durability:* Will the book fall apart with casual use or stand up to multiple readings?

Here's fair warning that this is a long chapter, with lots of detailed information—maybe more than you thought you wanted to know—about book printing choices and processes. But this is where the rubber hits the road in terms of your project: knowledge about printing-related issues will inform your design, your budget, and your timeline, and will make for a smoother process and a better final product.

THREE KINDS OF BOOK PRINTERS

As we've mentioned before, there are three kinds of book printers: print-on-demand (POD), short-run digital (SRDP), and offset. While POD companies market specifically to individuals, SRDP and offset printers primarily service professional publishers, who are notoriously cost- and quality-conscious. There is no doubt that the rise of POD companies such as Blurb and Lulu has created new opportunities for individuals and small organizations printing books. But POD printers offer virtually no customization, as well as far less consistent quality, than the two other options. And while it may be cost effective for very small runs of under 50 copies, POD quickly loses its value at higher quantities: the three types of printers are cost-effective at different run lengths, as the chart below shows. While the cost per book is highly contingent on the actual number

PRINTING COST PER BOOK: POD, SRDP, AND OFFSET PRINTING

64 page paperback, 10-¾ x 8-¼ landscape on 80-lb stock, four color throughout, printed proofs included for SRDP and offset, freight not included.

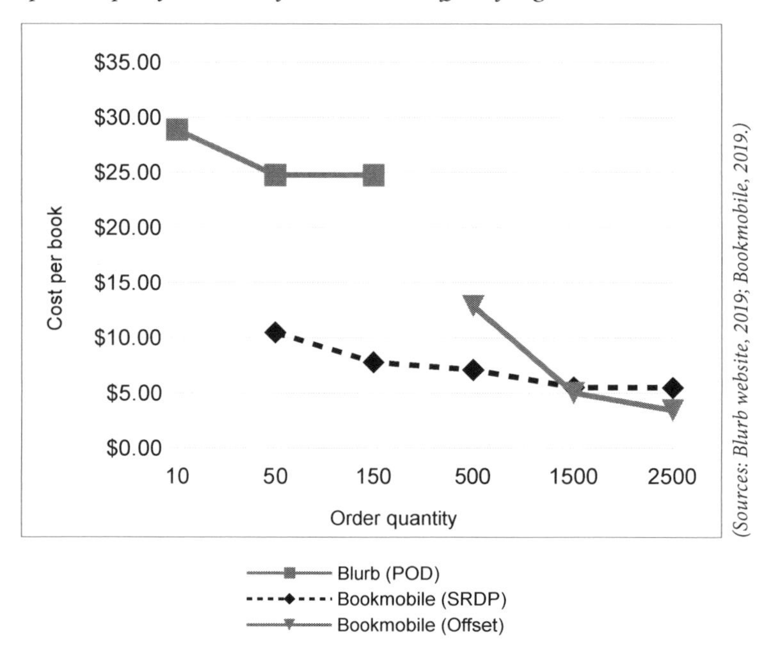

of pages, page size, binding, and so on, the chart accurately reflects the quantities at which each kind of printer has the best pricing.

Best pricing depends on quantity: POD is least expensive at small quantities, SRDP at medium quantities, and offset printing at longer runs. But price is not the only difference between the three types of book printers. In addition to substantial savings at larger quantities, SRDP and offset book printing can offer many more printing options, higher quality, and better customer service than POD.

Here are profiles of each type of book printer, showing their strong and weak points from the point of view of producing a fine art book.

PRINT-ON-DEMAND (POD)

- *Customer base:* POD printers such as Lulu, Blurb, and Bookbaby primarily serve individuals. They utilize digital printing equipment and automated order processing to print any quantity of books (even a single copy).
- *Workflow:* In running a book printing plant, every touch of a job by an employee adds to the printer's cost to produce the job. POD printers, with their tiny run quantities and low per-order billing, address this by automating everything possible, and excluding processes such as traditional printing proofs that involve labor-intensive interactions with the customer and add to production time.
- *Run lengths:* Because of automation, POD printers are generally unbeatable on price at quantities of 25 or fewer.
- *Quality:* Quality is generally pretty good, but short run lengths make quality control spotty because the companies cannot afford to do much checking for the low dollar amounts involved. Also, whereas SRDP and offset printers provide printed proofs for review prior to printing a book, POD printers are slam-bam: the finished books are the proofs. No proofs means no opportunity to make sure everything is as good as it can be prior to printing.
- *Page layout:* POD printers usually have their own software to enable individuals to create their covers and book pages, or they can take files—either native application files or PDFs—created with professional page layout programs such as Adobe InDesign or Quark Xpress.
- *Flexibility and options:* For POD, page sizes and printing options have to be severely limited in order to allow for maximum automation. For instance, with a POD printer you select the page size from the handful they offer rather than telling them what you want. Same with custom options

TEN WAYS TO SAVE ON PRINTING COSTS

1. LOOK AT THE TOTAL COST, NOT JUST COST PER BOOK. Because printing is always cheaper the more you print, the temptation to print more in order to get a lower price per book is ever present. But the true cost of printing per copy is not the total cost of printing divided by the number of *books printed*, it's the total cost of printing divided by the number of *books sold*. Those extra books cost real money to ship, to store, and, ultimately, to dispose of. Also, consider the cost of your time: A printer may offer $300 less on a run but be time-consuming and unreliable to deal with. And if the lowball printer screws up, they are *really* going to be a timesuck.

2. RIGHT SIZE YOUR PRINT RUNS. Crowdfunding makes estimating the number of books you should print a bit more rational, but it's still good to err on the conservative side. If you set the run too low, the worst case is that you have to reprint and may have a slightly higher printing cost per book. If you set the run too high—which is much more likely, based on the millions of books sitting unsold in warehouses—you will definitely pay the price.

3. DON'T PUT LIPSTICK ON A PIG. That's perhaps an unfortunate way to put it, but if the type of book you are publishing is strictly informational and not a work of art, don't go overboard on fancier paper, french flaps, and so on. Going fancy increases your costs while bringing no extra benefit to your readers. (This is not an argument against these options: they can absolutely be appropriate for some kinds of books.) See this chapter's section on printing options for more information.

4. SELECT THE RIGHT PAGE SIZE. Printing presses—both digital and offset—are optimized to print on certain size sheets or rolls of paper. The more pages that can be fit on those sheets without waste, the lower the printing cost overall. See this chapter's section on selecting page size for more information.

5. BE ORGANIZED TO AVOID COSTLY ERRORS. Keeping good records is crucial for guarding against mistakes that can cost a lot. Keep track of the details of the estimates you get, keep a paper trail of all communication you have with your designer, printer, and anyone else involved, and supply complete and timely information to avoid losing time, paying rush shipping charges, ordering the wrong quantity of books, or any of the other things that can result from poor recordkeeping.

6. GET QUOTES FROM THREE BOOK PRINTERS. Be sure to get quotes from book printers, not commercial printers. Printers specialize, and book printers are going to give you the best price because they have designed their plants totally around manufacturing books. Get quotes from three printers—even between book printers prices can vary for a particular project because their plants are set up differently. Because book printing is so competitive, it is generally a waste of time to get more than three quotes: printers know very well the pricing ballpark they need to be in.

7. SELECT PAPER FROM THE PRINTER'S HOUSE STOCKS. All book printers stock a range of book papers in different weights, shades, and quality. Choosing from this range, rather than specifying another paper, will save money because the printer buys their house stocks in huge volumes and can pass along that savings to you. Also, supplying paper to a printer can be tricky if you are not experienced in doing it: the printer is not responsible for any issues with the paper, and you will be stuck with the cost if there is a problem with it. If the printer supplies the paper, they are responsible. See this chapter's section on selecting paper for more information.

8. AVOID A RUSH JOB. Make sure you budget enough time to fulfill your backer rewards and have printed books on hand. Rush jobs often cost more in printing, because the printer may have to pay overtime or incur other costs. Also, rush jobs almost always cost more for shipping.

9. FOR 1,000 COPIES OR FEWER, GET QUOTES FROM DIGITAL BOOK PRINTERS; FOR 2,000 COPIES OR MORE, GET QUOTES FROM OFFSET PRINTERS. In addition to competitive pricing at 1,000 copies or fewer, digital book printers offer faster turnaround and much more flexibility in setting quantities of future reprints, which can save money. But if you need more than 2,000 offset printers can definitely provide lower printing costs—just make sure you really need that many books first. See this chapter's section on the three kinds of book printers for more information.

10. GET QUOTES FROM BOTH DIGITAL AND OFFSET BOOK PRINTERS FOR QUANTITIES BETWEEN 1,000 AND 2,000. In the range 1,000 to 2,000 copies, usually (but not always) offset book printers will be less expensive than digital book printers. Because of the other advantages of digital book printing—faster turnaround and flexibility for future reprints—it's worth pricing a run with digital printers as well as offset in this quantity range. They might surprise you with a better quote than offset, and then you get the other benefits of digital printing. See this chapter's section on the three kinds of book printers for more information.

like foil stamping, embossing, die cutting, custom endsheets, inserts printed on different paper, and so on: if they are offered at all they are strictly limited in material types and customization.

- *Customer service:* If it exists at all, it is likely to be extremely limited.
- *Pricing:* Lowest of all book printer types for quantities fewer than 50.
- *Turnaround:* Delivery times range from 7 to 11 days.
- *Sales and distribution:* POD printers typically have a web bookstore through which you can sell your books. Some also provide options for selling through Amazon and/or general distribution to the book trade. Fees vary, but are fairly transparent.

SHORT-RUN DIGITAL PRINTING (SRDP)

- *Customer base:* SRDP printers, like the industrial-strength POD printers, primarily serve traditional book publishers. However, for quantities from 50 to 1,500 they are usually the best option for photographers, galleries and other non-traditional publishers as well.
- *Run lengths:* SRDP printers produce quantities of 50 to 1,500 per order, either shipping the finished books to the publisher's warehouse or storing them in their own warehouse for future fulfillment.
- *Workflow:* While they often use the same kinds of digital presses as POD companies, SRDP printers' workflows are not oriented around totally automated hands-off production, but around producing small to medium

quantities of high-quality books at prices that work for super-cost-conscious publishers who also want lots of printing options. Service attributes that enhance quality and customer satisfaction, such as printed proofs and high-touch customer service, are maintained. While price quotes and order processing is likely to be highly automated, the actual production of the books is heavily hands on, with defined quality-control points for every task. The digital presses used are slower than offset presses, but produce book blocks that are ready for binding immediately without folding and gathering signatures. Binding machines are designed for fast setup, at the expense of fast production, because of the lower quantities produced per run compared with offset printing.

- *Page layout:* SRDP printers will expect you to provide print files produced in InDesign or Quark and will groan inwardly if you designed your book in Word or an amateur-oriented layout program, because these programs create a living hell for a printer with even basic expectations of quality.
- *Flexibility and options:* Because of the hands-on craft orientation of at least some SRDP printers, they can be much more flexible than POD printers. Here are some examples of what at least one SRDP printer, Bookmobile, can do that POD printers can't: infinitely customizable page sizes between the minimum and maximum sizes, flaps on paperbacks, printed endsheets, endsheets on custom paper stock, and book sections printed in color. While you are unlikely to need all these options, if you are producing a high-quality custom book that reflects the effort you have put into your photographs, you will likely want some of them. See the discussion of printing options later in the chapter for further details.
- *Customer service:* SRDP printers vary in their customer service approach: some go barebones, while others provide phone and email support.
- *Pricing:* The sweet spot as far as pricing goes for SRDP is generally 50 to 750 copies. From 750 to 1,500 copies, SRDP dukes it out with offset, and usually, but not always, offset wins for 1,500 copies or more. That said, which type of book printer is more competitive often depends on the specifics of the book being printed: there are cases where offset will kill SRDP at 600 copies, and, on the other hand, where SRDP beats offset at 1,500. When in doubt, quote with both.
- *Turnaround:* Delivery times for paperbacks range from 12 to 16 days, contingent on your approving proofs rapidly. Hardcovers will be longer.
- *Sales and distribution:* Bookmobile has its own distribution service, Itasca Books. For other SRDP printers you will likely have to sell the books yourself and/or arrange for selling through a book distributor. While the big

book distributors typically will not take on one- or two-book publishers, there are indie distributors that are happy to take on individual projects and provide an online bookstore like the POD printers as well as selling to Ingram, Baker & Taylor, Amazon, Barnes & Noble, and other sales outlets. See chapter 5 for more information about sales and distribution.

OFFSET BOOK PRINTING

- *Customer base:* Professional print buyers at publishing organizations, including museums. However, for long runs offset printing is also the best option for non-traditional publishers—photographers, galleries, museums, and others.
- *Workflow:* The workflow of offset book printers typically utilizes a high degree of automation in order quoting and processing, fast offset presses, and very expensive binding equipment optimized to produce large quantities of bound books. As with SRDP, offset printing plants incorporate proofs for the customer to review and approve, quality control points for every run, and customer service availability to help make sure things go smoothly.
- *Run lengths:* Until about 1996, virtually all books were printed at offset book printers in run lengths of 1,000 or more. Some of these companies wouldn't even quote pricing on quantities of fewer than 2,500. The upper limit is Harry Potter territory: millions of copies. We should all be so lucky.
- *Page layout:* Offset book printers will expect you to provide print files produced in InDesign or Quark, and, like SRDP printers, will groan inwardly if you designed your book in Word or an amateur-oriented layout program.
- *Flexibility and options:* Most offset book printers can offer a tremendous range of options for printing and binding your books. See the discussion of printing options later in the chapter for further details.
- *Customer service:* Offset printers, like SRDP printers, vary somewhat in their customer service approach, but most if not all provide phone and email customer service.
- *Pricing:* Offset printing is almost always the way to go for quantities of 1,500 or above. Between 750 to 1,500 copies, the specifications of a particular book will determine whether SRDP or offset is less expensive. Fewer than 750 copies is generally SRDP territory.
- *Turnaround:* Delivery times for four-color paperbacks will run 5 to 6 weeks. Add a couple of weeks for hardcovers. Printing in the Far East can take up to 4 months.

- *Sales and distribution:* If you use an offset printer you will likely have to sell the books yourself and/or arrange for selling through a book distributor. While the big book distributors typically will not take on one- or two-book publishers, there are indie distributors are happy to take on individual projects and provide an online bookstore like the POD printers as well as selling to Ingram, Baker & Taylor, Amazon, Barnes & Noble, and other sales outlets. See chapter 5 for more information about sales and distribution.

BEWARE: ALL OFFSET PRINTERS ARE NOT BOOK PRINTERS

An offset book printer is not the same thing as an offset commercial printer: don't expect to go to your local offset printer who does brochures and catalogs and expect to get the best price, or, for that matter, expect them to actually know how to produce a book. Successful offset book printers have been focused by extreme competition to be experts at their craft. That is not to say they are all equal, just that they are much more likely to give you good quality at a good price than a commercial offset printer is.

	Print-On-Demand (POD)	Short-Run Digital Printing (SRDP)	Offset
Best print quantities	25 or fewer	50-1,500	1,000 to 20,000
Quality control	Spotty	Good, depending on company	Good, depending on company
Pricing	More expensive after 50 copies	Lowest cost between 50-750 copies, generally	Lowest cost option 1,500 copies or above
Flexibility and options	Very little	Good, depending on company	Good, depending on company
Personal service	Minimal or none	Good, depending on company	Good, depending on company
Turnaround	7-14 days	2 weeks for first run, 1 week for reprints	4-8 weeks for first run. Can be seasonal.
Page layout	Website tools, InDesign, Quark	Indesign, Quark	Indesign, Quark
Workflow	Highly automated	Skilled craftspeople	Skilled craftspeople
Sales and distribution	Limited. Bookstores will not stock POD titles.	Yes, depending on company	Yes, through separate distribu-tion companies
Customer base	Individuals	Pros	Pros

THE UPSHOT

All this means that your best choice depends on quantity, quality, and your artistic vision for the book as embodied in the choice of materials, binding, and other printing options. If you only need a few copies of your book, and the page sizes and printing options of a POD printer are a good fit, go for it. If you need anything from 50 copies on up, or want tighter control of quality or more printing options, choose SRDP for up to 750 copies. If you're in the SRDP/offset overlap zone between 750 and 1,500 copies, get price quotes for both SRDP and offset. Over 1,500 copies, offset is almost always going to be your best bet.

The chart below sums up the differences between the three printing models.

PRINTING CHOICES

You have an almost unlimited number of printing and binding options available to you as a creator, but those options will quickly be filtered by the nature of your project. For example, if you're creating a poetry book, it is unlikely you will need to have a 12" x 12" page size. Conversely, if you've got a book of landscape photography a 4" x 6" page size is unlikely to meet your needs. Besides page size, similar considerations apply to binding, paper choice, and embellishments like foil stamping. The following section is a detailed discussion of making decisions about each of these options.

I. BINDING

The choice of binding is a critical piece of the publishing process. The right choice can help maximize title revenue and margins, while the wrong choice can

BINDING DEFINED

A **trade paperback** means a paperback book sold in a bookstore, as opposed to a **mass-market paperback**, which is the smaller size sold in drugstores and supermarkets as well as bookstores. Trade paperbacks are generally printed on better paper than the groundwood used in mass-market paperbacks.

A **hardcover** book may also be referred to as a **casebound** or **cloth** edition. They all mean the same thing: pages bound between hinged boards covered in cloth or special paper. Hardcover bindings come with a wide variety of options, from plain to extravagant.

Mechanical binding uses wire or plastic in coil or comb form to bind the pages and cover of a book together. Commonly used for applications where the book must lie flat, such as cookbooks and address books, mechanical bindings fare poorly in the book trade. Booksellers often decline to order books with such bindings because they are easily damaged by browsing customers and typically do not have a spine to display the title when shelved.

BINDING AND PUBLISHING STANDARDS

Though crowdfunded publishing projects obviously aren't operating under the same market forces as traditionally published books, it can be helpful to understand how those forces impact binding choices in the industry. Some books are published in multiple editions with different binding. The editions are released in sequence, highest list price to lowest, to maximize revenue to the author and publisher. Called "windowing," this is similar to the way that movies start at first-run venues with high ticket prices and move to cheaper-ticket theaters after the first run enthusiasm tapers off. With books, the theory is that for a big-name author there is a substantial audience of price-insensitive buyers who will purchase a hardcover at a premium price in order to read the latest and greatest. Following a year later, a less expensive trade paperback or mass-market edition (depending on the category) is released for sale to readers who will wait to buy the less expensive edition. In this way, revenue is maximized for the author and publisher.

A variant of this practice is the sale of paperback rights to another publisher subsequent to the publication of a successful hardcover first edition. Often, a smaller literary publisher with a hardcover success can make more money for themselves and the author by selling the paperback publication rights to a larger publisher rather than publishing the paperback themselves.

Windowing is getting trickier with Amazon preselling hardcover new releases at steep discounts, diminishing the market for the title at walk-in bookstores as well as for a subsequent trade paperback edition. Also, Amazon actively markets the lower eBook price as a "savings" over the print price for the same title. This is a battlefield for new titles, with publishers trying to hold the line on new-release eBook prices so they don't kill the hardcover market, and Amazon pushing to reduce eBook prices, regardless of what it does to publishers.

There are markets where delaying a paperback edition is irrelevant: university press monographs—published for a small audience of academics—are often released simultaneously in a hardcover edition for libraries and a trade paperback edition for sale to individuals. This is called a "split run." Also, libraries have their own requirements for binding. Because it is expensive for libraries to replace worn out books, libraries generally prefer hardcovers for their main collections. In fact, there is a whole category of businesses called "rebinders" that purchase books that are only available in a paperback edition and rebind them as hardcover specifically for sale to libraries.

diminish sales and increase costs. Awareness of the technical nuances in bookbinding can add value while keeping costs down.

Choosing the binding for your book is largely a marketing decision. Genre titles selling to readers who consume them serially and pay for them out of their own entertainment budget must have a low selling price, and therefore require an inexpensive paperback binding—or no binding at all, as an eBook. A medical reference title, on the other hand, might contain information critical to the practice of a high-paying specialty, so for consumers it will be a business expense, further reducing price resistance. The high price will easily pay for the additional expense of hardcover binding, and the hardcover binding itself reinforces the notion of high value.

So while other related factors have an effect on list price—such as an author's popularity or a specialist audience pushing prices higher, or public domain copyright status and category competition pushing it lower—binding type is strongly related to perceived value, as illustrated in this table:

Binding	List Price Range
Hardcover	$22.00–$200.00
Trade paperback	$12.00–$30.00
Mass-market paperback	$7.99–$11.99
Unbound (eBook)	$1.99–$14.99

Hardcover or Paperback?

In most cases, the answer is going to be trade paperback—not mass-market paperback. But aesthetic concerns or cultural significance may call for a hardcover binding if the budget allows for the more expensive binding irrespective of how many books are actually likely to sell. Bear in mind that hardcovers are physically larger and heavier than the equivalent paperback: not only will printing be more expensive, so will shipping and storage. (For more information about the processes of both paperback and hardcover binding, including definitions of the terms that appear in the tables below, see appendix F.)

Hardcover Binding Recommendations

The best hardcover binding technology choices are illustrated in the following table.

Type of book	Best digital printing option	Best offset printing option
Trade-sized hardcover; fiction, nonfiction	Adhesive casebinding	Adhesive casebinding; with some offset printers Smythe sewing may cost no more
Illustrated books with large page sizes	Print on uncoated stock and use EVA adhesive casebinding; or, use PUR adhesive casebinding	Smythe-sewn casebinding or PUR adhesive casebinding
Childrens books for library market, 24–48 pages	Side-sewn casebinding or PUR adhesive casebinding	Side-sewn casebinding or PUR adhesive casebinding
Childrens books for library market, higher page counts	PUR adhesive casebinding	Smythe-sewn casebinding or PUR adhesive casebinding

Paperback Binding Recommendations

The best paperback binding technology choices are illustrated in the following table.

Type of book	Best digital printing option	Best offset printing option
Trade-sized paperback; fiction, nonfiction	Adhesive perfect binding	Adhesive perfect binding; with some offset printers Smythe sewing may cost little more
Illustrated books with large page sizes	Print on uncoated stock and use EVA adhesive perfect binding; or, use PUR adhesive perfect binding	Smythe-sewn perfect binding or PUR adhesive perfect binding
Childrens books for library market, 24–48 pages	PUR adhesive perfect binding	PUR adhesive perfect binding
Childrens books for library market, higher page counts	PUR adhesive perfect binding	PUR adhesive perfect binding

2. PAGE SIZE

The page size of your book has an impact on every aspect of its publication: aesthetics, legibility, durability, cost, and perceived value. Choosing the right page size will keep printing costs down and minimize binding problems. Keep in mind that common trim sizes are usually the least expensive to print and bind. It generally does not pay to go to extreme trim sizes (books that are super skinny, super wide, or huge). They are less efficient and more costly to produce, less durable, and can cause logistical issues with packing, handling and displaying. See below for more information on the relationship of page size to printing cost.

The basic principal is that there is no reason to use a page that is bigger than necessary to achieve your aesthetic, legibility, and budget goals. That said, books whose purpose is to showcase images (such as art books) should have larger pages. Even if the images are reproduced at relatively small sizes, wide page margins will enhance the viewing experience. While in general larger page sizes are strongly preferred for image-heavy books, there are cases where you might use something smaller, such as compendia of artists' work (where the idea is to just give an impression of the work), or books showcasing art that is tiny to begin with (for which much enlargement beyond the original is inappropriate and could look awkward).

Aspect ratio is another consideration, and for books with images, the aspect ratio of the images should influence the aspect ratio of the pages. For vertically oriented images, a portrait format for the book is likely the best choice. If the images are mostly horizontal, a landscape format is preferred. If they are a mix of both vertical and horizontal, a square page can be optimal.

For portrait-format books, selecting the ubiquitous and boring 8-1/2" x 11" page size is an aesthetic trap. Change it up! Pick a size that fits press sheets economically but doesn't look like the same old letter size: 9" x 12" or 8-3/4" x 10". However, it's good to avoid extreme aspect ratios—not only can they complicate printing, but they can also create an aesthetically unpleasant reading experience (think about turning the pages of a very narrow, tall book: the narrow pages would feel stiff, fighting your fingers with every turn).

Landscape-format books have their own issues to be aware of. Landscape-format books are harder to bind, causing more waste and therefore incurring a higher printing cost. The extreme width of the page relative to the height of the spine creates leverage that stresses the spine, making landscape-format bindings more prone to damage than portrait-format books.

Some critical points to remember about trim size:

- Be sure and check with your printer before you design your book. A change of 1/8" in trim size could easily mean a difference in printing cost of 25 percent or more, while being aesthetically negligible. This actually applies to using any nonstandard trim size—see the discussion below on costs related to page size.
- Never sacrifice correct grain dimension to achieve a particular page size. You will be squandering any potential benefit of a custom page size by having a final book that is horrible to leaf through.
- Consider having the printer make a dummy book, which is an unprinted but bound book on the same stock and with the same binding as the final book. This dummy will cost money, but it could save thousands of dollars in helping avoid a design or production gaffe.

The Relationship of Page Size to Printing Cost

Printing presses—both offset and digital—are engineered around standard paper sheet sizes, or, in the case of roll-fed presses, roll widths.

Here's an example from a black-and-white digital press, the Océ VarioPrint 6320 Ultra. This press takes a maximum sheet size of 12.6" x 19.2". It can print 164 impressions per minute, which is 82 sheets per minute, given that each sheet requires two impressions. Four 6" x 9" pages can fit on one side of the sheet, with allowances for binding and trimming. This translates into 656 6" x 9" pages per minute.

Let's say that you wanted to use a slightly larger page size: 6-3/8" x 9". Since 6-1/2" x 2 is 12-3/4", greater than the 12.6" width of the largest sheet runnable on the press, only two pages could be printed per side. This means that only 328 pages could be printed per minute instead of 656. Since the cost of operating the press is the same whether you are running two pages per side or four, the cost of printing each page has doubled, even though the page width has only increased by 3/8". This consideration applies to all presses, as they all have maximum sheet sizes or roll widths.

Other considerations enter in as well. The larger pages would have to be rotated 90 degrees to fit on the sheet. Because the grain direction of the paper should always parallel the spine of the book, this means that a different stock of paper would have to be used for the printing. Also, printing only two pages per side means that either 1) paper is wasted by the poor fit of the pages to the sheet, or 2) a custom stock of paper must be trimmed down or ordered to run the job to minimize paper waste. In either case, costs go up: that 3/8" ends up adding significant cost to the printing.

Trim Size Recommendations

The best trim size choices for different kinds of books are illustrated in the following table.

Book characteristics	**Recommended Standard Sizes**	**Efficient Variants of Standard Sizes**	**Wider Format and Landscape Sizes**
Text-heavy	• 5-3/8" x 8-3/8" • 5-1/2" x 8-1/2" • 6" x 9"	• 5-1/2" x 8-1/4" • 6" x 8-3/4"	• Not recommended
Image-heavy	• 8-1/2" x 11" (Boring!) • 9" x 12"	• 8-1/2" x 10-3/4"	• 8-1/2" x 8-1/2" • 9" x 9" • 10-3/4" x 8-1/2"
Text- and image-heavy	• 8-1/2" x 11" (Boring!) • 9" x 12"	• 8-1/2" x 10-3/4"	• 8-1/2" x 8-1/2" • 9" x 9" • 10-3/4" x 8-1/2" • 12" x 9"
Poetry, short and medium-length lines	• 5-3/8" x 8-3/8" • 5-1/2" x 8-1/2" • 6"x 9"	• 5-1/2" x 8-1/4" • 6" x 8-3/4"	• Not recommended
Poetry, long lines	• 7" x 9"	• Not applicable	• 8-1/2" x 8-1/2" • 9" x 9" • 10-3/4" x 8-1/2"

3. PAPER

Like other production decisions, choosing paper (also referred to as "paper stock" or just "stock") affects the cost and aesthetic value of your book. When choosing paper, professional print buyers consider basis weight, thickness, color, finish and other factors in addition to cost.

Paper Density, or Basis Weight

The density of paper is expressed by basis weight. Basis weight is the weight in pounds of 500 sheets of the paper at a standard sheet size, which in the case of book papers is 25" x 38". For uncoated book papers, 50-lb., 55-lb., and 60-lb. are typical basis weights. Common coated stock basis weights are 70-lb., 80-lb., and 100-lb. In Asia and Europe, metric grammage is used instead of basis weight; instead of pounds, the unit is grams per square meter (gsm). By way of comparison, for text paper 60-lb. is roughly equivalent to 89-gsm.

Basis weight changes directly affect the weight of a book. A book printed on 60-lb. stock will weigh about 20 percent more than the same book printed on 50-lb. stock when the weight of the cover is factored out. Using 60-lb. stock instead of 50-lb. would therefore increase the cost of shipping a given quantity of the book. It may also increase the postage cost for shipping individual orders, depending on whether or not the weight of an individual copy is pushed into the next postage rate tier. Basis weight also affects the thickness (caliper—see below) of paper, although other factors enter into this as well, such as the method and amount of calendering used in the manufacture of the stock.

Paper Thickness, or Caliper

The thickness of paper is called caliper. Caliper is important because it determines the width of the spine of a book, and therefore the precise layout of the cover. Caliper is measured in pages per inch (PPI). The thinner the paper, the higher the PPI. For example, a 600-page book on 300 PPI paper will be 2" thick, excluding the thickness of the cover (600 / 300 = 2). A 240-page book printed on 360 PPI stock will be .66" thick, excluding the cover (240 / 360 = .66). The thickness calculated this way is often referred to as bulking.

Book paper should be consistently manufactured from batch to batch to a specified PPI, because the thickness of the paper determines the width of the spine. If the PPI changes significantly between batches when the book is reprinted the width of the cover spine will have to be changed to fit the altered bulking. This will take time and money, and may require another proof cycle, losing more time and introducing the potential for error.

Some uncoated stocks are manufactured to be thicker relative to their weight than standard stocks. These are called "high-bulk" stocks. High-bulk stocks are used to keep the weight and cost of the paper down while maintaining the same spine width as a heavier stock. For example, a 50-lb. high-bulk stock is 456 PPI, almost the same as a standard 60-lb. stock at 436 PPI. A book printed on the 50-lb. high-bulk has almost the same thickness as if printed on the 60-lb. stock, but weighs about 17 percent less.

Here's a list of typical uncoated digital book paper calipers:

- 50-lb. natural high bulk, 456 PPI
- 60-lb. natural trade book, 436 PPI
- 80-lb. white opaque smooth, 382 PPI

Papers used for books with very high page counts, such as bibles or fat computer manuals, are especially thin. Some have up to 1560 PPI.

Your printer can provide the PPI of the paper you are using to print your book for the purpose of estimating spine width, which will be important to the cover design. (See appendix A for information about calculating spine width.)

Opacity

Translucency in book papers is not good: It looks bad to have type or images on the back side of a page show through. Therefore, book papers are rated on opacity. Good book papers have high opacity. Opacity is governed by the caliper of the paper and the amount of pulp and fillers used in its manufacture.

Coated vs. Uncoated Papers

Papers are generally divided into coated and uncoated types. Coated stocks have been coated with materials to increase opacity, smoothness and ink hold-out when printed on offset presses. The materials used include naturally white minerals such as Kaolinite–the clay used to produce porcelain ceramics–or calcium carbonate, plus binders. Coated stocks are used in offset printing where high-quality image reproduction is required; on digital presses, reproduction may be better on smooth uncoated stocks. Coated stocks often come with different finish options—glossy, matte, or dull—which affect the reflectivity of the page. Coated stocks are heavier than uncoated stocks with the same amount of fiber because of the weight of the minerals used in the coating.

Commonly used EVA binding glues don't stick to coated stocks as well as they do to uncoated stocks, where they can permeate the fibers of the paper. Solutions are to use high quality opaque uncoated stocks—which may be preferable on digital presses anyway—or use a binder set up with PUR glue instead of EVA when binding coated stocks.

Paper Finish

As mentioned above, coated stocks are available in gloss, matte, and dull surfaces. Uncoated stocks used for book printing also vary in their surface finish, ranging from very smooth to vellum, which has a fine "tooth." For digital printing, the smoother the better. Novelty finishes such as "laid" or "cambric," which imitate handmade paper and fabric respectively, are almost never used for printing the text of books because of expense and printing quality issues. However, hardcover case cover materials—paper or synthetics—are readily available in different finishes, often imitating the texture of more expensive real-cloth materials.

Paper Color

Papers used in printing books typically come in shades of white or natural. Natural refers to cream-colored (as opposed to bright white) stock. Natural uncoated stocks are the standard for quality nonfiction and literary trade paperbacks. Natural stock connotes quality, and is reputedly easier on the eyes when reading for extended periods. Within the natural stock category, each type varies in shade, from light off-whites to darker cream colors. Ask for a sample from your printer.

White uncoated stock is used for illustrated books, textbooks, and within the trade paperback category, professional, self-help and how-to books. Coated stocks are mostly bright white, though each type varies in brightness. Some coated stocks are available in a light cream color.

Freesheet vs. Groundwood Papers

Paper is manufactured using either the freesheet or groundwood process. Groundwood is made of pulp created by mechanical grinding, which results in more impurities and coarser fibers. The impurities severely reduce the longevity of the paper. Groundwood is used in books where low cost is an absolute imperative, such as mass-market paperbacks. Groundwood is almost never used in digital book printing, because its dustiness causes maintenance problems and decreases the life of digital presses. Freesheet paper is manufactured with a chemical process that leaves it nearly "free" of impurities such as resins, lignin and groundwood fibers. It has a better finish and much longer life than groundwood stock.

In the 19th century, when advances in typesetting, printing, papermaking, and cheap rail transportation enabled a mass market for books, many books were printed on groundwood paper. In the early 20th century, it was discovered that these books were falling apart on library shelves: the acidic impurities in the groundwood literally caused the books to self-destruct. Book papers were improved by the free sheet manufacturing process, which reduces acidic impurities from the pulp. In addition, printers began to use alkaline buffers such as calcium carbonate to create an alkaline reserve within the paper, so that any remaining acidity was neutralized. Today, all quality book papers are "acid-free," so that libraries and other purchasers can be assured that books will not self-destruct on their shelves.

Recycled Papers

Paper is primarily made of wood fibers obtained by cutting down trees or using scrap wood. In addition, papermaking has always incorporated recycled fibers in the form of mill waste and scraps. Paper labeled recycled, however, incorporates recycled fibers from other sources such as discarded post-consumer waste. These post-consumer materials typically have to be de-inked before they can be used in making new paper.

Book papers with recycled content vary in price, availability, and printability. Recycled paper often has small flecks of color or other materials that may affect the appearance of the stock in a minor way. Generally, but not always, recycled stock is sold at a premium compared to regular stock, because obtaining the post-consumer fiber costs more than other sources of fiber. That said, it has been well documented that recycling paper reduces waste in landfills, saves forests, saves energy, and substantially reduces air and water pollution compared with using virgin pulp from cutting down trees. According to the EPA, recycling one ton of paper saves enough energy to power the average American home for six months, saves 7,000 gallons of water, and reduces greenhouse gas emissions by one metric ton equivalent.

Why You Should (Almost) Always Use Your Book Printer's House Stocks

Book printing is an extremely competitive business. A very large part of the cost of printing a book is the cost of the paper used, which the printer does not make and has to purchase from paper mills. Printers buy very large quantities of paper in order to get the paper at the lowest possible cost. The savings are passed along via lower prices resulting from a competitive marketplace.

Also, the papers that a printer keeps as their house stocks have been thoroughly tested and used for printing hundreds of titles: the printer knows that the paper prints and binds well. Book printers that use digital presses in particular have to be selective about what papers they use, as digital presses do not print well on many stocks with which offset presses have no issues.

Most book printers have a good selection of all types of papers commonly used for book printing.

That said, sometimes furnishing preprinted covers or special cover stocks can enable a unique creative element for a particular book. In these cases, success requires close collaboration with the printer, and you will likely be responsible for cover printing or binding problems, as the materials provided are produced outside of the printer's control.

Book Paper Recommendations

The best paper choices for different kinds of books are illustrated in the table below. Note that all papers listed are freesheet (permanent), unless specified as groundwood.

Book category	**Digital Press**	**Offset Press**
Trade fiction and literature	• 50-lb. high-bulk uncoated, natural • 55-lb. uncoated, natural • 60-lb. uncoated, natural	• 50-lb. high-bulk uncoated, natural • 55-lb. uncoated, natural • 60-lb. uncoated, natural
Trade nonfiction (history, public affairs, biography, etc.)	• 50-lb. high-bulk uncoated, natural or white • 55-lb. uncoated, natural or white • 60-lb. uncoated, natural or white	• 50-lb. high-bulk uncoated, natural or white • 55-lb. uncoated, natural or white • 60-lb. uncoated, natural or white
Other trade nonfiction categories (self-help, computer books, guidebooks, etc.)	• 50-lb. uncoated, white • 55-lb. uncoated, white • 60-lb. uncoated, white	• 50-lb. uncoated, white • 55-lb. uncoated, white • 60-lb. uncoated, white
High-quality illustrated books (art, photography, etc.)	• 70-lb uncoated, white opaque • 80-lb uncoated, white opaque • 100-lb uncoated, white opaque	• 70-lb coated or uncoated opaque • 80-lb coated or uncoated opaque • 100-lb coated or uncoated opaque
Other illustrated books (how to, textbooks, etc.)	• 60-lb uncoated, white opaque • 70-lb uncoated, white opaque	• 60-lb uncoated, white opaque • 70-lb uncoated, white opaque
Mass-market format	• Not recommended	• Groundwood, various weights

Other Paper-Related Considerations

TEXT INSERTS, OR GALLERIES

Often a book contains a handful of images in a sea of text. Those images can be laid out in special sections of the book called inserts or galleries. The inserts are printed on stock chosen to best reproduce the images—often a heavy coated or opaque white stock—while the text is printed on stock ideal for reading, such as a 60-lb. natural uncoated. Because the insert can be printed in full color while the body of the book is printed in black only, this can result in substantial savings over printing the whole book in color on the heavy coated stock. It also reproduces both text and images on their respective optimal stock. Offset printers, because they print in signatures of 4, 8, 16 or more pages, have limitations in the placement of inserts. Digital printers, because they print in single leaves of two pages each, can typically place an insert anywhere in the book. Multiple inserts can be bound into a single book.

PAPERBACK COVER STOCKS

Paperback covers are printed on stock that is coated only on one side, called, reasonably enough, "coated one side" or "C1S." The outside of the cover (the printed side) is coated to provide a good surface for color printing, and the inside is uncoated to provide the optimal surface for binding glue adhesion. Caliper (thickness) of these stocks is measured in points: one point equals 1/1,000". For most page sizes a 10-pt. C1S is an economical, high-quality choice. Larger page sizes—8" x 10" and above, and especially landscape format books—put much more stress on the cover. For these, use thicker 12-pt. C1S, or in extreme cases, 14- or 15-pt. C1S. Note that film lamination adds critical durability and tear resistance to paperback covers; UV coating and press varnish do not.

DUST JACKET STOCKS

Dust jackets are typically printed on C1S or C2S stock in the 80-lb. to 100-lb. basis weight range. As with paperback covers, the bigger the page size the more handling wear and tear occurs to dust jackets. The rule, therefore, is to use heavier dust jacket stocks for larger books. Film lamination is also as critical for durability for dust jackets as it is for paperback covers.

HARDCOVER CASE STOCKS

Hardcover cases can be covered with a variety of materials (paper, cloth, leather, etc.), and a range of finishes (smooth, cambric, fake leather, etc.) and colors. Your printer can provide samples. Most commonly used are paper cover materials in various colors and finishes.

ENDSHEET STOCKS

The endsheets are the folded sheets of paper at the front and back of a hardcover book. They are the hinges that attach the case to the book block. As such, they have to be strong and are typically an 80-lb. stock. "Matching" endsheets are the color of the stock chosen for the text. Otherwise, endsheet stocks, like case cover stocks, are available in a huge range of colors. Endsheets can also be printed in either color or black and white; printed endsheets are one of the ways that a hardcover book can be dressed up.

4. EMBELLISHMENTS

From the very beginnings of book printing hundreds of years ago, printers have added artistic embellishments to printed books. In fact, the very first printed books were designed to look like hand-scribed manuscripts, complete with hand-inked colored capitals and marginal decorations. Centuries of bookmaking have added to the options available, including:

- Foil stamping
- Blind embossing
- Sections of text pages printed on different paper stock, perhaps in full color
- Fold-out inserts
- Flaps on a paperback
- Dust jacket on a paperback
- Printed endsheets in a hardcover
- Endsheets in paperbacks, printed or on special stock
- Three-piece hardcovers (front and back cover with one kind of covering, with cloth on the spine)
- Many more!

If you're working with a designer, they may incorporate embellishments into the design; browse around in bookstores and online for ideas. Remember that POD printers don't offer this sort of customization, but SRDP and offset printers should be able to give you an idea of all the options they can offer. And of course, remember that any of these cool features is going to affect your printing (and potentially, your shipping) costs.

STAGES IN WORKING WITH A PRINTER

It's important to note that the real communication between you and your printer happens in quote requests, quotes, job confirmations, proofs, and so on. Anything communicated by phone may as well have not happened. The book printer will more than likely insist that all decisions and instructions on your part be communicated in writing: this is for your benefit as much as for theirs!

STAGE I: QUOTE REQUEST

Due diligence dictates getting three quotes—more is a waste of time (see "Ten Ways to Save on Printing Costs" in this chapter for more on that, and also "Three Kinds of Book Printers" for more on which type of printer to get quotes from). But before you can actually write a printing quote request, you need to know what you want. A printer can do nothing with the question "How much does it cost to print a book?" any more than a builder can answer the vague question "How much does it cost to build a house?" Books, like houses, vary tremendously in terms of the amount of work required to make them and the cost of materials.

So get specific. Narrow down your specifications to at most three total combinations of binding, paper, and page size, with the page count determined by the manuscript length. Resist the temptation to request quotes on any more than three combinations: more will sabotage your decision-making, not help it. Trust us on this: trying to consider too many combinations will mess with your head.

Sample Printing Quote Request

<table>
<tr><td>Title:</td><td colspan="2">War and Peace</td></tr>
<tr><td>Quantities:</td><td colspan="2">250 / 500 / 750 / 1,000 — +/- 5% overs/unders</td></tr>
<tr><td>Trim size:</td><td colspan="2">6" x 9"</td></tr>
<tr><td>Pages:</td><td colspan="2">864</td></tr>
<tr><td>Cover original:</td><td colspan="2">InDesign application files with all fonts and high-resolution images placed</td></tr>
<tr><td>Cover printing:</td><td colspan="2">4c process one side plus gloss lay-flat film lamination, with bleeds, on 10-pt. C1S</td></tr>
<tr><td>Text original:</td><td colspan="2">Print-ready PDF</td></tr>
<tr><td>Text printing:</td><td colspan="2">Prints black on 55-lb. natural, no bleeds</td></tr>
<tr><td>Binding:</td><td colspan="2">Perfect bind and trim</td></tr>
<tr><td>Proofs:</td><td colspan="2">Printed proofs</td></tr>
<tr><td>Packing:</td><td colspan="2">Bulk in doublewall cartons</td></tr>
<tr><td>Shipping:</td><td>Proofs to:
L. Tolstoy
21st Century Press
123 Blue Avenue
Zanesville, Ohio 43701</td><td>Books to:
Sellmore Distributors
48 Fortune Avenue
Webster, Wisconsin 54893</td></tr>
<tr><td>Need quote by:</td><td colspan="2">Tuesday, January 20th, 2020</td></tr>
</table>

The most intuitive way to constrain your choices is to simply pick a book in the same genre as yours and use it as a model in terms of page size, paper, and so on. There is no shame whatever in this: there have been thousands of wonderful books published in similar boring old page sizes on similar paper: their wonderfulness is not because somebody chose a wacky and expensively inefficient page size or an exotic paper, it is because of 1) what's in the book, and 2) the designer's imagination in working within the constraints of a generic format. The guidelines for Binding, paper, and trim size discussed in the previous section should help, too.

Because the number of possible variables are huge, we'll use this example of a simple paperback quote request, discussed point by point below.

Everything on this quote request is essential information, and there is no information missing. Email this along with a brief note to your contact at the printer and you're good to go. Don't bother explaining what your book is about—this is all about printing, not publishing, not editing, not literary criticism, and not promotion. The person estimating your printing is awash in books of all kinds. Don't take it personally, but they could care less what your book is about. They do care a lot about whether they get your printing work and, assuming they are a quality book printer—as opposed to an online print-on-demand mill—about doing a good job printing your book.

Let's go through the items one by one:

TITLE: You have to provide one, because otherwise how will everybody keep straight which quote is for which book? A working title is fine. If you're doing a couple of variations, identify that in the title: *War and Peace* (paperback), and *War and Peace* (hardcover). Or, *War and Peace* (60-lb natural text stock), and *War and Peace* (50-lb. natural text stock).

QUANTITIES: Often you're going to want to see pricing at different quantities: list them clearly here. The "+/- 5% overs/unders" indicates that you're willing to accept up to 5 percent fewer books ("underruns") or 5 percent more books ("overruns") than the order quantity. The printer will then charge you a reduced rate for overruns to the specified amount or credit you for underruns. Offset printers almost always require allowing overs/unders: the reason is that there is always waste in printing and binding, and hitting an exact quantity is almost impossible. The overs/unders clause allows the printer some leeway in production while at the same time ensuring a reasonable deal for you.

TRIM SIZE: As you know by now, trim size means page size (it is called trim size because it is the final size the book block is trimmed down to). See the earlier discussion about trim size for guidelines about how to select the best size for your book. On the quote, width is always listed before height: 6" x 9" means six inches wide and nine inches high. 9" x 6", on the other hand, means nine inches wide and six inches high—a landscape-format page, which will be significantly more expensive to print and bind. If you really want a landscape format book, be redundantly clear:

Trim size: 9" x 6", landscape.

PAGES: Pages in a quote request means the total number of all pages: printed pages, blank pages, Roman-numeraled frontmatter pages, and Arabic-numeraled body pages. They all count. Also, the page count must be an even number because every sheet of paper has two sides—at least in this universe! Because offset presses print multiple pages on large sheets which are then folded into signatures the page count often must be rounded up to a number divisible by 8 or 16, with the extras being blanks at the end of the book. Digital presses, on the other hand, normally print so that the page count can be any number divisible by two. Often printing quotes are required before the book has actually been typeset, and therefore before the page count is known. Calculating the page count for this purpose is called making a castoff. Note that even the most carefully calculated castoff is an estimate: in the huge majority of cases the final page count is different than that of the castoff. What this means is that the printing estimate calculated from a castoff will change when the actual page count is known: the initial estimate is only a starting point in the budgeting process. Please note that the printer cannot calculate your castoff for you—that should come from your designer, or from you if you're going DIY. See appendix A for how to estimate page count with a castoff.

COVER ORIGINAL: Cover original is the format in which you are supplying the cover to the printer. This is more standardized than it used to be, consisting normally of an application (Quark or InDesign) file along with all required fonts and hi-res image files, a PDF file, or both. If you are supplying something else—a piece of flat art to scan, or, God forbid, a Word file—tell the printer. These formats require much more work on the printer's part: you'd better find out up front if the printer is going to charge more as a consequence.

COVER PRINTING: This key piece of information tells the printer how you want the paperback cover printed, on what kind of paper stock, and what kind of coating (lamination, UV, none) you want applied to the printed cover. A typical paperback cover is printed in four-color process on the outside only, on 10-pt. C1S stock, and laminated. Other cool options may be available as well, such as foil stamping, French flaps, blind debossing, and so on. Talk to your designer and the printer about options.

TEXT ORIGINAL: As with the cover, you need to tell the printer how you are going to furnish the text pages to them. A print-ready PDF is usual, but you can also supply pages to scan, either as loose pages or as a bound book. In either case, scanning is more labor-intensive and therefore costly, and if the bound book cannot be cut up for scanning, it will cost even more, as each page has to be scanned slowly by hand.

TEXT PRINTING: Text printing indicates the parameters of printing the pages: ink colors, paper stock, and whether the printing bleeds—that is, runs off the edge of the page.

- *Ink colors:* As we discussed earlier, except in super-rare instances, ink colors are either black (black and white, in other words), or four-color process (meaning images can be printed in full color). You can also specify the text pages to be printed in black, with designated groups of pages—inserts—printed in color, either on the same stock as the main part of the text or a different page stock. If the majority of your pages print in black but some print in color, using inserts can save a considerable amount over printing the entire book on a four-color press. Note that inserts must have an even number of pages, and at an offset printer, they may also need to have a minimum number of pages. Here's an example of how the text printing for a book with two inserts would be specified: 160 pages black on 60-lb. natural, no bleeds; plus 8 pages 4c process on 80-lb. white matte-coated, bleeds; plus 12 pages 4c process on 80-lb. white matte-coated, bleeds. In offset book printing, inserts must fall between signatures of the main text pages; with digital book printing inserts can fall between any two pages.
- *Paper stock:* See the earlier discussion of paper for guidelines on choosing the right stock for your project; but in general, choose from the printer's house stocks to keep costs down, rather than specifying the paper from a paper merchant's catalog.
- *Bleeds:* Running the printing off the edge of the page—"bleeds"—requires additional prep work and can require printing a book with fewer pages per sheet or on a bigger press, either of which results in higher cost. However,

it may or may not cost extra for a particular trim size and paper stock at a particular book printer: be sure and indicate if your pages bleed to get the most accurate quote possible. If a book is quoted without bleeds and then furnished to the printer with bleeds, you may get a big upcharge.

BINDING: For a typical paperback, the normal specification would be "perfect bind and trim" or "perfect bind," which mean the same thing. The other typical option would be "casebind" or "casebind and wrap dust jackets," with the case materials and any options—foil stamp on front, foil stamp on spine, blind embossing, headbands, and so on—spelled out in detail.

PROOFS: When the printer receives your original materials, they will prepare proofs that show as much as possible how your book is going to print without actually putting it on press. You should see proofs both for the cover and for the text. Any real book printer will furnish proofs adequate for you to do the necessary checking. Digital printers will furnish proofs produced on the actual presses that will print your book, which are therefore more accurate representations of how your final books will look. Be aware that it is not possible to evaluate color for proofing purposes on a computer screen.

PACKING: Book printers can pack your books in different grades of carton, and they can shrink wrap your books prior to putting in the cartons as well. Shrink wrapping is not normally done for books destined for bookstores, except for expensive art books. In fact, it can be a detriment to selling to bookstores. If you plan on shipping full cartons via UPS, request double wall cartons to avoid future headaches and loss of sales from damaged books.

SHIPPING: Any book printer can give you pricing for shipping a given quantity of books by a given shipping method to a specific address *with zipcode*. If you have multiple destinations, indicate the number of books going to each. If the shipping destination has a loading dock, spell that out in your shipping instructions: with larger shipments the printer may be able to save you money by shipping via LTL, but *only* if the destination has a loading dock, delivery is not to a residence, and you do not request a lift-gate on the delivery truck. Also—very important—indicate where the proofs will be shipped and by what method. All of these details are critical to 1) getting an accurate shipping estimate, and 2) allowing the printer to figure out the most cost-effective way to ship your books. See chapter 5 for more on fulfillment and distribution.

NEED QUOTE BY: If you don't specify when you need the quote it will go into the queue for normal handling and delivery to you at an unspecified time—a few days, a week, whatever, depending on the estimator's workload. If you need it by a specific time, say so here. Be aware that to a printer, a publisher whose quotes must always be rushed signals a publisher who doesn't plan, is disorganized, and therefore will be more costly to work with.

Many printers have portals where publishers can request quotes online, and even order printing. These can save time by presenting the printing specifications as multiple-choice options and often by producing quotes instantly. Check with your book printer to see if such a portal is available for your use.

STAGE 2: QUOTES

The printer prepares a quote based on the specifications provided by the publisher (you) in the quote request. The quote is really where the chain of custody starts. The printer restates the specifications of the book as provided by the publisher and provides pricing. The printer is committing to print the book at the specifications stated in the quote—not any other quantities or bindings the publisher and printer may have discussed—contingent on receiving clean print files. Because memory is fallible, and people who prepare quotes are fallible, it is critical that you review each detail of the quote and make sure that the specs are correct. If they are not correct, the publisher should have the printer revise the quote to reflect the desired specifications. The quote protects the printer by specifying exactly what they will do for the price named, but it also protects the publisher. The printer can't claim later that the price is $3.50 per book if they specified $2.75 per book in the quote.

If specifications change (page counts, shipping requirements, etc.) between the time a book is initially quoted and the time finished books are shipped, pricing will change. It's important, therefore, that you get up-to-date quotes when specifications change, at least if they are major changes. Refer to the last quote by number when submitting a request for a quote revision: it will speed the quote revision up and make it more accurate than if the printer has to start from scratch for each revision. It is also super-important to review and keep all the quotes in the series: sometimes publishers do not track the effects on pricing that changes to specifications produce and then have a very unhappy surprise (why are surprises usually unhappy?) when they get the final invoice.

Once you've gotten multiple quotes, choose the printer that offers the best fit. And remember, the best fit isn't simply a matter of the lowest cost per book:

choosing a printer who lowballs a quote can end up costing you in other ways. (See "Ten Ways to Save on Printing Costs" in this chapter.)

STAGE 3: PRINT ORDER

When you're ready to print your book, you submit a print order. The print order is your written order to the printer to commence printing. When the printer has the print order and the print files in hand, production can begin, but not before. Also, the printer can only provide a firm schedule with both print order and print files in hand, because they have no control over when the print files will arrive. In the case of an exact reprint with no changes to cover or text, a print order alone will suffice because the printer has the files in their archives.

The print order should specify quantity and shipping instructions, should echo back all the specifications of the book being printed, either explicitly or implicitly by referencing the quote number and date, and should make note of any special requests or important information like events tied to the book. Note that without accurate shipping instructions, a printer really can't provide an accurate price or an accurate schedule. Late shipping instructions are often the cause of late books: regardless of when the book is actually completed, it cannot be shipped without shipping instructions.

STAGE 4: ORDER CONFIRMATION

When the printer receives the print order, they will carefully review the order and identify any discrepancies with the original quote. If something needs to be checked or revised, they will communicate with you. If all looks in order, they will volley back an order confirmation outlining the general specifications of the order, including quantity, and referencing the quote. As with all the other steps, this is another opportunity to catch any errors. The order confirmation is the printer's restatement of their understanding of the project. Make sure it squares with your understanding! Is the order quantity correct? Is it the right book? (There are lots of similar-sounding titles in the world!) Are all the specs correct? Let the printer know immediately in writing of any issues—put yourself on record and avoid later problems.

If all of this repetition seems redundant, that's because it is, and that's exactly the point. As with language and computer communications protocols, built in redundancy ensures accuracy, if all parties play their roles.

STAGE 5: PROOF REVIEW

When you send your print files to the printer, they are run through the preflight department, which tries to catch all-too-common issues in the files, and then to a proofing department, which will use a specialized workstation, called a Raster Image Processor (RIP), to produce the final files that will actually be used to print your books. In the case of Print-on-Demand (POD) printers, the preflighting is automated and no proofs are supplied; the files are printed, and the books bound and shipped to you. Because no proofs are supplied, you have no further opportunity to check how the images in your book are going to print. You'll see when you get the finished books (at which point, of course, it is too late to make any changes or corrections). Short-run digital printers (SRDP) and offset printers, on the other hand, provide proofs for you to check as a matter of routine, and in fact will require that you sign off on proofs before they print the books. The purpose of proofs is to demonstrate to the publisher exactly how the book is going to print. However perfect the files the publisher supplies, bad digital things can happen due to software issues or operator error. The proofs represent the book pages and cover after the printer performs whatever internal magic is required to print. The proofs will also display any bad things that were in the files when they were provided to the printer. In both cases, proofs provide the opportunity to catch and rectify problems before the books are printed and bound.

Proofs are also a commitment to you on the part of the printer, essentially saying, "Here's how the book is going to print. If it doesn't print like this it is our responsibility to remedy the issues." Conversely, it is also a statement by the printer to you: "You'd better check this carefully, because this is how the book is going to print, and if you find something you don't like after we print it, we're still going to bill you for the run."

The printer's responsibility is to print the files as they receive them with maximum fidelity. Even if the files contain an obvious typo, it is your responsibility, not the printer's. The printer should flag the typo if they notice it, but they are not obligated to find the error in the first place. On the other hand, if there are no typos, the printer is obligated not to introduce any, and is responsible for fixing any runs where they do introduced typos.

Proofs can be printed or electronic. In either case they should accurately represent how the pages and cover are going to print. Obviously, electronic proofs will never look the same as the book looks when actually printed on paper: viewing on screens and paper are different physical and physiological processes entirely. Also, with proofs for offset printing, there are some limitations: proofs are not usually printed on the presses that will actually be printing the books, because it is cost prohibitive. Instead, they are printed on digital devices that have varying degrees of fidelity to how the actual books will look. Digital book printing has the advantage that proofs can be printed on the actual presses that will print the final run, providing the best proof fidelity possible within the day-to-day variances of presses.

As with the previous steps, the proofs are opportunity to nip problems in the bud before they wind up stacked on a pallet. Interior proofs should be checked page by page to ensure that the book will print as desired. Cover proofs should be checked element by element: errors on a cover or dust jacket are particularly conspicuous and embarrassing. If reviewing printed proofs, the ideal method to indicate corrections is to write them on the actual proofs and return the proofs to the printer, along with a list of pages with corrections to be made.

Proofs are not, however, a place to edit the book. Corrections or alterations made at this stage are probably 50 times more expensive to make than they would be if made before the print files were provided to the printer.

Along with the proofs, the printer will send a proof transmittal with three options, as follows:

- *OK to print as is:* This means that you have carefully reviewed the proofs and see nothing that needs to be corrected. This commits you to the run, just as the printer is committed to print the books to match the proof exactly.
- *OK to print with corrections indicated made:* This generally means that there are a few corrections to be made but that you trust the printer to make the changes prior to printing without checking the corrections yourself. If the printer goes ahead and prints after the publisher signs the proof transmittal this way, then the printer is responsible for having made the corrections. (If the printer has questions about the requested corrections, they need to straighten that out prior to printing, or be liable for any errors.)
- *Make corrections indicated and provide new proofs:* This means there are things that need to be fixed, which you have marked on the proofs, and you want to see new proofs after the changes have been made. Unless the corrections are really minor and you've worked with the printer before, this is definitely the safest option.

Just to be insistently redundant: "OK to print" means OK to print as is with no changes. You have checked the proofs and every single thing is perfect as far as you are concerned. This protects both you and the printer. If the printer prints and binds the book and the final book is wrong in some way that *did not* show on the proof you approved, you are in a position to negotiate for a reprint or credit depending on the severity of the issue. Conversely, if you review the proofs and indicate "OK to print" and there is something wrong with the finished books that *did* show in the proofs, you are not going to get any reprinted books or credits because you didn't flag it in the proofs for correction. This means you need to really, really check the proofs, not just glance at them and say "OK to print." NOTE: For information specific to checking proofs of full-color images, see appendix D.

Despite these checks and balances, mistakes can be made: As long as there have been printers and publishers, there have been errors on both sides of their transactions. Also, there have always been things that publishers find in proofs that they want to change. Consequently, specific terms have come into being to refer to the responsibility for these changes. If an error found in proofs was clearly caused by the printer, it is called a Printer's Error (PE); the printer is obligated to fix PEs at no cost to the publisher. An Author Alteration (AA, sometimes called a Customer Alteration, or CA), is a change the publisher requests to the text or layout after the printer has started working on the project. The alteration may be requested because a typo was not caught prior to submitting the print files, or because an editor wants to reword something: it doesn't matter, it

KEY THINGS TO CHECK ON PROOFS AND ORDER DOCUMENTS

The following are things with which we often see problems, and should definitely be on your list of things to check in quotes, orders, order confirmations, proof transmittals, and so on. These are NOT the only things you should check: these are just the highest-risk items.

FOR BOTH COVERS AND INTERIORS

- Does the title and author name on the front cover, spine, and back cover match the title and author name in the interior of the book and vice-versa? Are they spelled correctly?
- Does the ISBN on the back cover match the ISBN on the copyright page?
- Is the trim size of the cover the same as the trim size of the interior?
- Does the width of the spine fit the bulk of the interior pages?

COVER

- Is the bar code on the cover and does it scan?
- Is the cover stock and lamination correct?
- Is the color correct?
- Are the type and images legible?
- If the cover is printed on the inside, is the inside cover included?

INTERIOR

- Is the interior stock correct?
- Are the type and any images legible?
- Are all pages present?
- Are the margins correct?
- Are the fonts and line breaks correct?

is chargeable to the publisher because it is a responsibility totally outside that of the printer's ambit.

In the days when printer not only printed but set the metal type, each AA was billed individually. There are examples from 19th century authors such as Dickens and other who totally rewrote the text on the page proofs, which, in the days of hand-set type, would mean many (billable) hours of AAs. A big profit center for the printer! Nowadays, if alterations are to be made, normally the publisher makes the changes themselves and submits new print files. Instead of charging per AA, the printer will just charge flat fees for redoing all the file prep and providing new proofs.

STAGE 6: SHIPPING DOCUMENTS AND INVOICE

Oh, glory day! The books are done! Now the printer ships them and provides tracking information. Depending on the shipping method, you can track their journey to the degree your obsessions require. The final invoice is prepared either right before the book ships or immediately after. As with previous documents, the invoice should echo the basic details of the print run: title, quantity, and so on. The pricing should match the quote. You should review the invoice as carefully, as all the other documents in the production chain of custody.

STAGE 7: INSPECTING THE BOOKS

As you may have gathered, printing books is a process that has a significant potential for error, both on your part and on the part of the printer. You must inspect the books when you receive them so that if there are any issues they can be resolved quickly. It does no good to go back to the printer three months later: waiting will only complicate the process, and in some cases—like warped books or bad packing—it will be impossible to substantiate to the printer because they have no idea what has happened to the books since they left their plant. So open a carton and check for major stuff. Be aware that book printing is a manufacturing process and therefore there will be variability between books, which your ultimate readers will never notice because they are not comparing copies side by side. The questions to answer in this inspection are obvious things: Were the books bound with the pages right side up and in order (yes, sounds stupid, but it happens)? Are there significant marks or dirt on the pages? Is the color within a reasonable range of the proofs you approved? Are there missing pages? Basic stuff.

If something is screwed up, take a deep breath. If it's your fault, deal with it: accept the books as is or make the corrections and reprint, at your expense. If it's the printer's fault, document it: refer back to the correspondence you saved (remember you were going to save all the correspondence with the printer?). Sometimes, to be frank, when the correspondence is reviewed it turns out it was your fault after all: deal with it, as outlined above. If it is the printer's fault, talk to the customer service or sales person about this issue—if it is not a matter of nitpicking about normal manufacturing variations on your part, they should do something about it.

This all may sound kind of negative, but it is part of the real world process of ensuring quality. Most of the time by far, if you put the effort into the process as we've described, you're going to get great looking books.

CHAPTER 5

FULFILLING YOUR BACKER REWARDS AND POST-CAMPAIGN SALES

As we've said before, the hardest part about publishing a book is getting the book into the hands of readers, and this is a big part of what makes crowdfunding so useful for publishing projects. Kickstarter and other crowdfunding platforms allow you to market your book in the course of your fundraising campaign. Backers are your initial audience: they fork over support (money) in return for first-run copies of your book. You spend money on printing only after you have found the initial audience for your book—your backers. This is a far more rational model than traditional book publishing. The kicker is that you can still market and sell your book through traditional means after you fulfill your backer rewards. And, unlike the book trade, where you're lucky to get 35% back, your backer dollars have no middlemen nibbles taken out except the Kickstarter and credit card fees, which are much smaller than the discounts taken by distributors, wholesalers and retailers.

FULFILLING YOUR BACKER REWARDS

You can fulfill your backer rewards yourself, have a fulfillment service do it, or, in the case of Bookmobile at least, have the printer do it.

Many crowdfunding publishers fulfill their own backer rewards. They have the books shipped to them and then pack them and ship them. This is very doable, if onerous. You have to purchase packing materials, pack the books securely—you don't want them damaged in shipping after all that work!—address the packages, figure postage, and get everything to the post office. The more successful you are with your campaign, the more work all this is. One pitfall to be aware of is underestimating how many international backers you'll get and the cost of shipping their rewards to them. This comes up over and over again in creators' accounts of their crowdfunding experience. Also, freight from the printer to you can be tricky. If you're printing up to about 500 books they will likely be shipped from the printer via UPS and can be delivered to your home or anywhere else with a street address. If you print more than that it can be much less expensive to have your printer ship on pallets via LTL (less than truckload) freight services; in fact, offset printers almost always ship this way. LTL freight lines, however, only deliver to facilities with truck docks: if you have them deliver to a residence you'll see delays and big "inside delivery" charges, and you'll likely have to do a lot of schlepping of heavy cartons.

There are a several fulfillment services which specialize in fulfilling backer rewards. You have the books shipped to their facility and they take care of receiving the books, storing them as long as necessary, and shipping them to backers. They'll charge for all of the above, plus postage, of course.

Bookmobile, which also handles both shipping and fulfillment, can provide all the services a fulfillment service does in addition to actually printing the books. If you choose, Bookmobile can also sell your crowdfunded book to the book trade on your behalf. You'll likely see savings because you don't have to pay freight from the printer to the fulfillment service. Bookmobile can also help you estimate the cost of shipping both domestic up front when you are planning your project, which can be very useful in setting your campaign target.

After you've fulfilled your backer rewards, there are several channels you can use to continue selling your book, if you're interested in reaching a wider audience than your initial backers. Later in this chapter, we'll talk about direct sales options. But first, here's what you need to consider if you want to sell your book through book stores.

SELLING THROUGH THE BOOK TRADE

Selling through bookstores is complicated, risky, and, frankly, not very profitable for publishers unless they publish a lot of titles every year so that they have a few financial successes to carry all the others. Nonetheless, in the United States, most books get sold this way, as follows:

1. A publisher signs an agreement with the author of the book to publish it. The publisher designs, edits, and markets the book.

2. The publisher contracts with a book distributor to sell the book to bookstores and book wholesalers. Because the network of wholesalers and booksellers is called "the book trade," the distributor who serves these markets is called a "trade distributor." The biggest publishers do their own distribution.
3. If a wholesaler buys the books, they in turn sell it to their customers, who are bookstores and other retailers who sell books. Bookstores, who obtain books both directly from the publisher and from wholesalers, sell them to consumers.

The key idiosyncrasy of the U.S. book trade is that books are sold on a returnable basis, meaning that a bookstore can return them for full credit to the wholesaler or publisher. A wholesaler can also return books to a publisher for full credit. This means that a publisher might get orders from bookstores and wholesalers for 2,000 copies of a new book, and have absolutely no idea how many are actually going to sell and how many will be returned for credit. The books that are returned will often be shopworn and not salable as new books. The publisher still absorbs the cost of printing those books, as well paying for shipping them to and fro. It can easily take up to a year for a publisher to know how many books have actually sold, as they trickle back in the form of returns.

Because of returns, selling through the book trade is much more risky than providing books as rewards to Kickstarter backers and selling direct yourself at events, through your website, and perhaps as an Amazon merchant. In addition, you make much, much less when you actually do sell a book through the book trade because all the middlemen—distributors, wholesalers, and bookstores—take a percentage of the sale at every step. Compare the profit when you sell a $20.00 book direct yourself versus through the book trade in a typical transaction:

In this example, which is not atypical, the publisher (you) makes only $4.20 on average for a trade sale, compared with $19.35 for a direct sale; and that $4.20 has to cover the cost of printing the book (including the copies that were returned unsold), paying for design and editing, and so on.

So, you have been warned: selling through bookstores is really, really tough. If you do chose to do it, here are the main differences from a budgeting point of view.

The sales model now includes selling into the book trade as well as selling direct, which means that you wind up with two or more selling prices (retail and wholesale). Also, because selling to the trade requires going through a distributor, you'll need to factor in the distributor's fees.

Selling Direct		
Selling price	$20.00	
S&H you charge	4.00	
Total sale	**24.00**	
Less postage	-2.65	
Less fullfilment cost	-2.00	
Publisher	**$19.35**	(before paying for printing, publishing costs, etc.)

Selling Through Book Trade		
List price	$20.00	
Bookstore cut	-8.00	(40% of list)
Wholesaler cut	-3.00	(15% of list)
Net sale	**9.00**	
Distributor cut	-1.80	(20% of net sale is on the low side)
Cost of returns	-3.00	(30% is average)
Publisher	**$4.20**	(before paying for printing, publishing costs, etc.)

Because the book trade publishing model includes a huge uncertainty about how many books are actually going to sell (since stores can return unsold books for credit), and because the middlemen take so much out of the sale, you have to focus on reducing the cost per book for printing. This means printing more books right off the bat and printing at an offset printer. It also means more risk and not much flexibility in terms of reprints. Instead of printing being a cost that varies with the number of books you actually sell, it really becomes a fixed cost, because you're going to have to print several thousand to get the cost down.

Because selling through the book trade requires informing so many more people about your book in order to drive sufficient sales to make the money part work, the marketing portion of the budget is pumped up in this example. (Remember, by the way, the above calculation is only an example, and you're going to have to figure out the most accurate estimates you can for all these budget items.) Selling several thousand books through the book trade is really hard.

For a sample Title P&L worksheet that includes selling to the book trade, see appendix B. In this P&L, books are sold directly by you in person or through your website, as well as through trade channels. Be aware that if you sell through trade channels, the retailers—especially Amazon—will likely discount the price so that nobody will want to buy from your website for full price. That's part of the price you pay for selling through the book trade. The no-revenue copies for backers and staff are also included, because doing so facilitates keeping track of total number of copies required.

SELLING DIRECT TO CONSUMERS

Yes, the Internet and Amazon have indeed shrunk the odds of selling your book profitably in the book trade to about the same as winning the Powerball. But they have also enabled new book sales possibilities, entirely separate from the traditional book trade channels:

- Selling on your own website direct to readers.
- Selling on Amazon, *but only as an Amazon merchant*, *not* as a regular book supplier.
- Selling in the back of the room at speaking engagements and other author appearances.
- Selling in bulk to organizations with a reasonable discount, nonreturnable.
- If selling to bookstores, doing so *only* at a 50% discount, non-returnable, paid with a credit card.
- Selling any other way you can for cash on the barrelhead, not allowing returns, and discounting as little as possible.

So here's what utilizing these options might look like:

- You create, edit, and design the book, and mount your crowdfunding campaign.
- You promote the hell out of the book, driving as many links as possible to your campaign page to reach potential backers.
- You promote the hell out of the book some more.
- Once you've reached your goal, you can either print via SRDP or offset, depending on how many backers you have.

  If you have fewer than 1,200 backers:
  You should print a first run at an SRDP printer to cover your backer rewards and supply you with a small additional quantity. With an SRDP printer you can reprint in small quantities as necessary. Printing SRDP will cost more per book than if you print 2,000 copies with an offset printer, but the odds of selling 2,000 copies of any particular new title are tiny. If the book does take off, you can always go back for a long run at an

offset printer. If it doesn't take off, you still have a chance to make money because of the higher profit margins of this model (as opposed to selling through bookstores), and because you didn't waste your precious project capital on printing too many books.

If you have 1,200 or more backers:
You should most likely print offset: compare pricing both ways.

- After you've fulfilled your backer rewards, you sell books through your website, again promoting the book like a mad person and driving as many links as possible to your website.
- You exploit your author platform like crazy, selling books at personal appearances.
- After a month or so, when you have likely maximized your sales through your website, you sell the book on Amazon through your Amazon merchant account. (Not through a distributor or Amazon Advantage!) You set the selling price. Amazon collects the money, including shipping & handling, and deducts about 15% of the sale price. Your book gets pretty much the same exposure on Amazon as any other book except for those by splashy big-name authors.
- You keep promoting the book in every way you can come up with.
- You reprint your book when you get close to running out. The goal here is to never pay to print books that you can't sell, because those books will likely be the biggest drag on your overall profit from the project. (Plus they will be a constant nagging message of failure, justified or not!)

Now, not every element of this model may work for you as an individual publishing a book. Setting up a website to sell a single title is a pain, for instance, and works much better if you have multiple titles to spread the cost over. And self-promotion is not everybody's cup of tea. (Heads up, though: promotion is *the* key to getting books in the hands of readers.) Maybe your project by its nature does not have a wide audience. Regardless, by utilizing the model above you will take control of the publishing process rather than letting it be dictated by the ponderous schedules and procedures of the book trade. And you have much better odds of making a profit.

DISCLAIMERS

First, you shouldn't think that any of this is easy. Any publishing project is a lot of work, no matter what business model you use. But if you are serious about your publishing project, this business model is almost certainly a more rational way to publish than the old book trade model, or, for that matter, through a POD service. And direct sales are a natural complement to crowdfunding.

Second, if you can definitely sell 2,000 copies, then offset printing, not SRDP, is going to be the way to go. Just don't under-estimate how hard it is to sell 2,000 books!

Third, if you are famous, the old-fashioned trade publishing model *may* be your best route.

CHAPTER 6

CREATING AND DISTRIBUTING EBOOKS

eBooks have grown from less than one percent of book sales in 2007 to about 20 percent in 2014. However, eBooks don't sell equally well in all categories, but are concentrated in fiction—especially genre fiction. In the U.K., for example, over 45 percent of eBook sales consist of crime, fantasy, and romance titles. The catch-all category that includes illustrated books—as well as graphic novels, science/nature, food & drink, children's nonfiction, and others—comprises less than 10 percent of sales.

Part of this is surely due to the fact that while the experience of reading fiction on a device is not that different than reading on paper, the experience of browsing a beautifully printed and bound picture book is of a different order than flipping through pictures on a screen. But there are also barriers to publishing illustrated eBooks that don't exist for books that are primarily text.

In any case, if you're interested in tapping into this market with your crowdfunded project—whether you're crowdfunding the creation of the eBook itself, or considering converting the book to an eBook after you've crowdfunded a successful print run—this chapter covers the basics of creating and distributing eBooks.

EBOOK ECONOMICS

Because there are no printing or shipping costs for eBooks, the economics are pretty simple. There's the up-front cost of creating the eBook. This can be $0 if

EBOOKS AND QUALITY

There are thousands of garbage eBooks on Amazon because it is so easy to publish through the Kindle platform. For a while, authors who were only concerned about making money kept making shorter and shorter e-"Books" in order to get the most revenue for the least effort. (Amazon has responded by changing payment terms.) Sometimes they didn't even write the books: there have been plenty of cases where people copied and pasted somebody else's content and published it as their own. Readers are not stupid; once burned they will shy away from anything that looks amateurish, as they come to expect not only poorly edited—possibly pirated—text, but terrible formatting and other production attributes. This is why eBooks published by traditional publishers continue to sell, and at much higher prices than self-published titles: readers can expect that the books are real books, that they are professionally edited and designed, and they have at least a basic level of readability.

This is not at all to say that all self-published eBooks are worthless; on the contrary, some have a quality level equivalent to a book published by a traditional publisher. In those cases, though, the author invested time and dollars into good design and editing, not to mention the fact that they wrote a good book to begin with. (To be honest, many of these authors had, in addition, already been published by traditional publishers and so had already crossed the basic quality hurdles.)

The upshot: don't think of an eBook as a shortcut. If you've got the time and the skills, you can DIY a lot of the process of creating an eBook. If you have any doubts about that and you want to stand out from the self-published crowd, it may be worth it to invest in hiring pros: have the text of your book edited (if you think you don't need an editor, you're mistaken), have it professionally converted to eBook format, and get a professional cover design.

your book is simple and you DIY using the tools available at Amazon or eBook services. Hiring someone can cost $200 to over $1,000 depending on the complexity of your book and the quality provided. Once the eBook files are made they are uploaded to the resellers: Amazon, BN.com, Kobo, and so on. The resellers pay for each sale minus their fee, which ranges from 30 to 55 percent of the selling price.

eBook services and publishing services such as Bookmobile can provide eBook creation services either standalone or in combination with distribution to the resellers. These services can sell eBooks through many more outlets than is practical for an individual, including Amazon, BN.com, Kobo, library suppliers and international outlets. They charge separate fees for creating the eBook and for distribution.

Because Amazon is the primary seller of eBooks, a common strategy for self-publishing authors is to sell exclusively through Amazon. This has the virtue of simplicity, and Amazon sometimes pays a higher royalty. However, this means forgoing selling through other outlets. Also, read the fine print on Amazon's publishing programs: some authors have done very well, but Amazon has the right to change the royalties paid and does so regularly, to the chagrin of a lot of self-publishers.

The rest of the chapter discusses the options for creation and distribution of eBooks in more detail, but first, let's look at the different kinds of eBooks you can make.

TWO KINDS OF EBOOKS

eBooks come in two flavors: reflowable and fixed layout. eBooks comprised primarily of text are almost always reflowable, meaning that the reader can change the size and style of the type. Indeed, that is one of the benefits of reading an eBook! With fixed layout, eBooks type sizes and other aspects of page layout cannot be altered by the reader: pages are displayed as they were designed by whoever created the eBook file. In many cases, fixed layout eBooks mirror the design of the print edition of the book exactly. Books can be converted into *either* reflowable or fixed layout eBooks. Each has its advantages.

REFLOWABLE EBOOKS

Positives

- Will display on many more devices than fixed layout eBooks.
- Less time-consuming and therefore less expensive to create than fixed-layout formats.
- On the appropriate device—i.e., the iPad with Retina screen—image reproduction can be excellent.

Negatives

- The design of the book is totally lost.
- On monochrome eBook reading devices, image quality is atrocious.

FIXED LAYOUT EBOOKS

Positives

- Pages can be fully designed, like a print book.
- Image display on appropriate devices can be excellent.

Negatives

- Time consuming and expensive to create because each page has to be individually laid out, just like a printed book.
- To reach the whole eBook market, three versions must be created, because each of the major eBook sellers—Amazon, Apple, and Barnes & Noble—has

a different fixed layout file format. Therefore even more expense will be incurred compared to a reflowable eBook.

Based on the evidence in the marketplace, the conclusion that many publishers come to is that if you're going to create a fixed layout eBook, do it for the premier viewing platform, the iPad—the expense of conversion for smaller-screen devices is not worth it.

WAYS TO CREATE EBOOKS

Companies that offer publishing services can create your eBook, whether it is reflowable or fixed layout. See appendix C for a partial listing of such companies. If you have the time and inclination, you can create your own eBook.

REFLOWABLE EBOOK CREATION TOOLS

Here are tools that can be used to create reflowable eBooks:

- Adobe InDesign
- Pages
- PressBooks

Be aware that none of these tools create a finished eBook! Even using InDesign, the resulting files must be tweaked and tuned to actually work with the various eBook resellers' reading software. Publishing services companies should test the eBooks they make on each of the major devices, using an XML editor called Oxygen to modify the files so that they work properly.

Also, be aware there are two major reflowable eBook formats: Kindle (Amazon) and EPUB (everybody else). The great tool Calibre will convert from EPUB to Kindle; as always, you'll have to actually test the file on a Kindle once you convert it and you will likely have to tweak the EPUB so that it converts well to Kindle.

FIXED LAYOUT EBOOK CREATION TOOLS

Following are descriptions of the tools that can be used to create fixed layout eBooks.

Adobe InDesign

Adobe exports to a fixed-layout EPUB 3.0 file. Expect to do substantial testing and editing. Programming experience will help. eBook reader compatibility with the fixed layout features of EPUB 3 is minimal, so it is a big question whether it is even worthwhile to attempt it.

Kindle Publisher Tools
This is for creating eBooks for Amazon Kindle, including KF8 format fixed layout eBooks. Note that Kindle's fixed layout implementation is designed primarily for textbooks and children's books.

iBooks Author
This creates fixed layout eBooks only for the iPad, with an option to enable the reader to switch between reflowable and fixed layout. It also has built-in widgets for things like image galleries, and you can create your own widgets. In addition, there is rich support for audio and video media. If you are targeting the iPad with your fixed layout eBook, this is your best bet.

The PDF Workaround
Of course, there is another way altogether to create a fixed-layout eBook, and that is to create a PDF of the print files of the book. The eBook pages will match the print edition exactly, and the cost to create the eBook will be minimal. PDFs can't be sold through the major eBook resellers but can be readily distributed through your website if you don't care about having the file copy-protected. There is also a way to apply copy-protection—aka digital rights management, or DRM—utilizing Adobe Content Server, but setting up an account with a service providing the Adobe DRM is cost-prohibitive for just one title. For more information on DRM, see the next section, about eBook distribution.

CONCLUSIONS

If you're publishing a romance or mystery, creating an eBook version in addition to—or even instead of—a print version is a no-brainer. With art and photography books, it is a much tougher call whether it will be worth the effort and expense. Should you decide to proceed, it is worth considering whether to just publish for the iPad using iBooks Author, instead of spending the money to attempt to sell on platforms not so well suited to displaying high quality pages and images.

DISTRIBUTING EBOOKS

Self-publishers have multiple options to create and sell eBooks. Though Amazon is the 900-pound gorilla in the eBook world, a lot of eBooks get sold through other channels. Here's a snapshot of eBook retailer marketshare:

eBook Retailer	Marketshare
Amazon	79.5%
Apple iBookstore	13.0%
Barnes & Noble	3.0%
Kobo	2.0%
Libraries	2.5%

(Source: Bookmobile, 2018.)

In addition, library wholesalers such as Overdrive and Ebsco sold the equivalent of about 2.3 percent of the retailer volume, and new wholesalers—3M, Brainhive—have come online.

Other published statistics do not match the above exactly (some show Barnes & Noble with a larger share, Amazon with a smaller share, etc.). However, from the point of view of maximizing your eBook sales, the moral is the same: if you're selling only through Amazon, you're likely reducing your potential sales by about 30 percent. The tradeoff is time and effort—each sales channel you add takes more time to manage and will involve creating new eBook files. You have to balance the effort required against the potential revenue. For self-publishers, access to channels is limited to those that support self-publishing. However, as the top four—Amazon, Apple, Barnes & Noble and Kobo—comprise around 97 percent of the market according to our stats and others, and they all support self-publishing, that's not a big deal. Another alternative is to work with an eBook aggregator, rather than with the big resellers individually.

EBOOK AGGREGATORS

eBook aggregators can help reach more sales channels. They provide services to self-publishers similar to what distributors provide to traditional publishers: they can create eBook files for you, distribute eBooks to retailers and wholesalers, and pay you the money they collect for sales of your eBook. You just provide your book text and information to the aggregator, and you don't have to provide it to each reseller individually because the aggregator does that for you. That can mean a considerable time savings. Aggregators charge setup fees and/or a percentage of sales revenues for their services. See appendix C for examples of some eBook Aggregators (if you do a Google search on "self-publish eBook" you'll see plenty more).

TWO SELF-PUBLISHING STRATEGIES

Keeping in mind the balance of effort vs. revenue, there are a couple of viable strategies for selling self-published eBooks:

- use the self-publishing services of each of the top four eBook resellers, or
- use an eBook aggregator to distribute to the top four plus other channels.

In both cases, you'll reach at least 97 percent of the market. With an eBook aggregator you'll spend some money, likely save a bunch of time, and reach a bunch of channels you couldn't otherwise reach, including libraries.

WHAT YOU NEED TO SUPPLY

Whether you are working with an eBook aggregator or dealing with the major resellers yourself, you need to provide these four things:

- The eBook file itself
- A cover image
- Title information, aka metadata
- Banking information

The earlier part of this chapter offers detailed information about creating eBook files—here's some information on the other things you'll need.

Cover Image

Despite the fact that eBooks have no physical covers, the cover image is critical for marketing the book. The absence of a cover image signals to buyers that no effort has been put into the book. Secondly, the quality of the cover design matters. Readers interpret the quality of the cover image as a representation of the quality of the book: an amateurish cover signals an amateurish book, a professionally-designed cover signals a professionally designed and published book. People definitely do judge a book by its cover—if you've created a great book, don't shortchange your effort with a lousy cover.

If you have design expertise, it may not be a big deal for you to produce a cover image. If you don't, you would be well advised to hire a professional graphic designer (see chapter 2 for more information about working with a designer, who in this case you'd be hiring just for the cover). eBook aggregators will also design a cover image for you. From what we've seen these designs vary a lot, from slapdash to pretty good.

Cover images are produced in Adobe InDesign or Adobe Photoshop and exported as JPEG files in the dimensions specified by each store for uploading. If you use an aggregator, you should only have to produce the image at one size and the aggregator will resize it for the various sales channels.

Title Information, aka Metadata

Metadata is all the information about the eBook that appears on the sales page: title, author, description, editorial reviews, price, ISBN, author bio, and so on. (Note that each edition of a book, including eBook editions, need their own unique ISBN.) Metadata is critical to telling your readers what your book is about. Given that they will only buy your book if they can tell what it is about, it's pretty important. Some elements of metadata are simple (the title, the author's name, and the price, for example). Other elements—the description, any sales handles, author bios—need to be well-written, because they are critical for reader's decision-making process. Study the descriptions provided for the top-selling paid books on Amazon: those are the ones produced by traditional publishers, who put a lot of effort into writing book descriptions. Have the description edited.

If you use an eBook aggregator, you'll have to put the metadata in just once, and the aggregator will distribute it to the various sales channels. If you work directly with the major resellers, you'll have to put the metadata into each of their systems yourself.

Banking Information

When you sign up to sell your eBook, the other party—whether an aggregator or a big reseller—has to have a way to pay you. For most of them, this means a direct deposit to your bank account. Therefore, you'll have to give them banking information so they can do this.

SELLING EBOOKS FROM YOUR WEBSITE

Selling eBooks from your website seems like a dream business: no printing costs, no picking and packing, no postage to deal with. Plus, you're connecting directly with readers in a way that you can't when you sell through an intermediary like Amazon or Apple. If you are doing direct-to-reader sales already with your print book, selling eBooks can definitely be worthwhile.

But there are complications. First, you need to have sufficient traffic to your website to generate real sales. Just adding eBook sales to an otherwise static, low-traffic website is unlikely to be worth the effort. Second, the question of whether or not to utilize Digital Rights Management (DRM) is a thorny one.

THE BENEFITS OF SELLING EBOOKS DIRECT TO CONSUMERS

The clearest benefit to selling eBooks direct is the increased revenue per sale. Selling direct means that you're not giving a share of the sale price to Amazon or another reseller. This can mean 50 to 100 percent more revenue per sale, depending on your current arrangement with resellers.

Perhaps just as important, when you sell direct, you get the customer's contact information, including their email. With their permission you can add them to your mailing lists and keep them in the loop for any future projects.

DRM OR NO DRM?

Digital Rights Management (DRM) is what prevents readers from freely copying eBooks and giving them away, or, much much worse, putting them on a pirate download site where potentially thousands more can get your book without paying for it. From the point of view of most publishers and authors, this is uncontroversial: why should they enable pirates to steal the hundreds of hours of work on the part of the author and the investment the publisher makes in the book? Publishing is a risky and not particularly profitable business even without piracy. But it is not quite that simple. There are many vocal anti-DRM voices on the web. Granted, most of them have no skin in the game: they argue from abstractions, having not spent years in writing the books in question or invested in their publication. But there are actually publishers that argue against DRM, including computer book publisher Tim O'Reilly. Here are the arguments against DRM:

- DRM inconveniences readers by preventing them from moving the eBook they legitimately purchased onto different devices, or reselling them.
- DRM facilitates the extension of monopoly power on the part of big resellers, Amazon in particular, by corralling your rightfully purchased content in a "walled garden" where you will be inclined to return when you want to make more purchases.
- Piracy, rather than depressing the sales of particular books, actually encourages it because the hardest thing to do in publishing is making readers aware of your book. According to this theory, free copies floating around raise awareness of books among people who will actually buy them.
- While DRM prevents legitimate users from casually making copies, it doesn't really prevent the real bad guys: there are software tools out there to crack every DRM, including those for eBooks.
- Information just wants to be free. Especially, it seems, information created by the sweat of somebody else's brow.

With all due respect to Tim O'Reilly, these arguments are mostly balderdash. Anyone who has purchase and read eBooks from Apple, Amazon, Barnes & Noble and Kobo would be hard-pressed to say they've actually been inconvenienced. Reading an eBook by its nature is like reading a cheap mass-market paperback, which is basically disposable. Nobody is buying eBooks to put on a bookshelf to treasure forever. eBooks are inherently less valuable than printed books, if more convenient. The argument that piracy generates sales is unprovable: All you know for certain is that you didn't get paid for the pirated copies. And finally, the argument that the results of intellectual labor ought to be free just because the cost of reproducing it is low is persuasive mainly to those who build empires on revenue generated by free content or by acquiring customers via free content to sell them something else (think of Apple or Amazon)—or perhaps to academics whose salaries are paid by other means.

So, we are generally pro-DRM. For someone selling eBooks direct from their own website, however, DRM is a challenge. There is only one generally accepted technology for doing so, Adobe Content Server 4 (ACS4). But the associated costs of acquiring and using this technology (in the tens of thousands of dollars) make it out of reach for any self-publisher.

An alternative is to sign up with an eBook fulfillment service using ACS4. (See appendix C for a partial listing of companies that provide this service.) This reduces the setup costs drastically, to a couple of thousand dollars, and eliminates the need for you to set up dedicated servers just to sell eBooks. Because this service includes not just the furnishing of DRM but the fulfillment of the actual eBook files to your customers, the cost is around $0.50 per book in volume.

SELLING EBOOKS WITHOUT DRM

Given the complexity and expense of setting up and operating ACS4, even some publishers sell eBooks without DRM. eBooks can be added to an eCommerce website as a downloadable product. Customers can add them to shopping carts and pay for them just as they pay for a physical book. After they check out, the eBook is provided instantly as a download. Pretty simple. Another nice thing is that while ACS4 doesn't support Amazon Mobi-format eBooks, it's just as easy to sell them without DRM as it is to sell ePubs or PDFs.

The risk is, of course, that your files will make their way to a piracy site and harm legitimate sales.

So, you have three choices for selling eBooks from your own website, either of which may be uncomfortable:

- invest upwards of $40,000 to implement ACS4 and hundreds more a month to operate it
- sign up with an eBook fulfillment service such as Bookmobile provides, with an initial investment around $2,000, or
- sell without DRM.

Any of these options must be seriously evaluated against the probability of generating sufficient revenue to make it all worthwhile and against the risk of piracy.

CONCLUSION

Go for it. That's the conclusion. This little book is full of best-way-to-proceeds and more than a few pitfall-warnings, and when it came to write a conclusion I thought at first I would attempt to make a pithy summary about book-making "best practices." But the ultimate "best practice" is in fact just that: practice. Sure you'll run into snags, but what creative endeavor is free of challenges? Learn what you can from our experience, as expressed in these pages, but don't let any of this suggest your project isn't worth doing, or that you can't do it. After all, we learned how to make books by—you guessed it—making books. You can too. *Go for it.*

APPENDICES

APPENDIX A: CALCULATORS

BOOK WEIGHT

For an online calculator, visit the Bookmobile website (https://www.bookmobile.com/book-weight-calculator/). Read below for directions on how to estimate your book's weight yourself. Note that weight calculated this way is rarely spot-on, but it's important for estimating shipping costs when you are budgeting a book project, especially if you are sending out single copies.

The weight of a book depends on these factors:

- Number of pages, including roman-numeraled frontmatter and any blanks.
- Page size.
- Paper density, as measured in basis weight (U.S.) or grammage (metric).
- An allowance for the cover weight.

Here's a simplified formula for calculating the weight of a paperback using basis weights.

$$\text{Book weight} = ((\text{Basis weight} \div 950{,}000) \times \text{Page width} \times \text{Page height} \times \text{Page count}) + .06$$

Where:

- Basis weight is the standard measurement of the paper's density. The "basis weight" of a 60-lb. stock is 60 lbs.
- 950,000 is the number of surface square inches in a ream of text stock at the basis weight sheet size (25" x 38").
- .06 is an allowance for the weight of the cover, glue and lamination. This is based on a 6" x 9" book with a 1" spine: you can nudge this value up or down for larger or smaller page sizes.

Here's an example. A book has 316 pages, and is to be printed on a 60-lb. paper stock, with a paperback cover printed on 10-pt. C1S (coated-one-side) stock and laminated. The book's page size is 6" wide by 9" high. Let's calculate the weight step by step:

$$\text{Weight} = ((60 \div 950{,}000) \times 6 \times 9 \times 316) + .06$$

$$\text{Weight} = 1.0778 + .06$$

$$\text{Weight} = 1.1378 \text{ lbs.}$$

As with inches, a decimal value for pounds isn't very useful, but it is easy to convert to ounces by multiplying the decimal fraction by 16:

.1378 x 16 = 2.2048 oz.

Rounded: 3 oz. (Always round up: that's what UPS and the USPS will do!)

Add back in the whole number from the decimal weight calculated above and you get:

Book weight = 1 lb. 3 oz.

SPINE WIDTH

For an online calculator, visit the Bookmobile website (https://www.bookmobile.com/book-spine-width-calculator/). Read below for directions on how to estimate your book's spine width yourself. The spine width of your book is important to know because it allows you to accurately lay out the cover file for printing. The spine width of a paperback book is dependent on three things:

- The number of pages, including roman-numeraled frontmatter pages and blank pages.
- The thickness of the paper, expressed in pages per inch (PPI). Your printer should provide the PPI for any paper they quote printing on.
- An allowance for the thickness of the cover. This allowance should also be provided by your printer. We use .0156", which assumes the cover is printed on 10-point C1S (coated-one-side) stock, the standard, and is laminated.

The formula for calculating spine width is:

Spine width = (Pagecount / PPI) + Cover thickness allowance

Here's an example. A book has 316 pages, is to be printed on a 400-PPI paper stock, and the printer has given you an allowance of .0156" for the thickness of the cover. Let's calculate that step by step:

Spine width = (Pagecount / PPI) + Cover thickness
Spine width = (316 pages / 400 PPI) + .0156
Spine width = .79 + .0156
Spine width = .8056"

A decimal value for inches isn't very useful, but it is easy to convert to fractional inches by multiplying the decimal fraction by 32 to get the spine width in 32nds of an inch:

.8056 x 32 = 25.779 16ths

Round 25.779 to 26 and you get 26/32", which simplified is 13/16", so

Spine width = 13/16"

Because binder tolerance is around 1/32" and actual paper thickness varies with humidity and temperature, rounding to the nearest 32nd of an inch is fine. Your printer should fine tune the spine width if it is necessary, without you even asking: you can check the result on the cover proof they provide.

The same formula works for high page count books as well. Here's an example. A book has 840 pages, is to be printed on a 400-ppi paper stock, and the printer has given you an allowance of .0156" for the thickness of the cover. Here are the calculations:

Spine width = (Pagecount / PPI) + Cover thickness
Spine width = (840 pages / 400 PPI) + .0156 cover thickness
Spine width = 2.1 + .0156
Spine width = 2.1156"

Multiply just the part to the right of the decimal point by 32 to get fractional inches:

.1156 x 32 = 3.6992 16ths

Round the 32nds:

3.6992 32nds rounded is 4/32", which simplified is 1/4"

Add in the whole number to the left of the decimal point (the 2 in 2.1156):

2 + 1/4 = 2-1/4" spine width

In the U.S., hard cover boards usually add about 1/4" to the width of a spine, so this same 840-page book would have a spine width of 2-1/2" as a hardcover:

2 + 1/4 + 1/4 = 2-1/2"

This is useful for sizing foil stamp art for the spine, but dust jackets are notoriously tricky to size because of the joints at the spine and the way that jackets wrap around the boards. We highly recommend getting dust jacket measurements from your printer. You can also do this for your paperback covers.

PAGE COUNT

As we noted in chapter 4, page count estimate created before a book is actually designed is called a castoff. "Estimate" is the operative term here; castoff page counts are only estimates and will almost certainly vary from the actual, final page count. However, they are much better than guessing for the purpose of preventing unpleasant printing cost surprises late in the project. The usual process is to get printing quotes using the castoff page count, and then get revised quotes once more accurate page counts are available after page layout.

For an online calculator, visit the Bookmobile website (https://www.bookmobile.com/book-page-count-calculator/). Read below for directions on how to estimate your book's page count yourself.

For text that runs page to page, such as the chapters of a novel or a nonfiction book, the number of pages is determined by how much text will fit on a page. How much text fits on a page in turn depends on the size of the area on the page devoted to holding text—known as the "type page"—as well as the size of the type and spacing between the lines. There are two methods for making castoffs using the number of characters in the manuscript and more or less precise estimates of the number of characters that will fit on a page:

1. Use a rule of thumb characters-per-page value to calculate the text page count.
2. Calculate the characters-per-page value used to figure the text page count using information about the specific typeface to be used for the book.

These methods use character counts for calculation purposes. Character counts are more accurate than word counts because the average number of characters per word varies by author, subject matter, and language. One author might have an average word length of five characters, another six: that's a 20 percent difference in calculated book length! Microsoft Word and other word processing programs will give you character counts for your manuscript document. The character count should include spaces, by the way.

THE LIST OF ELEMENTS

It is good practice to make a list of all the elements in the book when you do your castoff. This helps ensure you don't forget something, which is useful for simple books and absolutely necessary for big, complicated books. Here's an example of a list of elements for a novel:

- Bastard title page
- Blank
- Title page
- Copyright page
- Dedication
- Blank
- Chapters
- Blank
- Blank
- Author note
- Blank
- Colophon

I'll expand upon this sample list of elements as we look at castoff calculation methods. This list, by the way, is useful not just for the castoff but as a tool in organizing the production of the book. As far as what elements your book should have and where they should go, the Chicago Manual of Style (https://www.chicagomanualofstyle.org/home.html) is an invaluable resource.

CASTOFF METHOD 1: USE A CHARACTER COUNT RULE OF THUMB

Here's a rule of thumb for calculating the amount of body text in a book based on average per-page character counts for various page sizes. This method is not as accurate as method two which uses specific font metrics, but it is better than nothing if you just need a rough estimate.

1. Divide the total number of characters in the book by a typical number of characters per page for the planned page size.
2. Add in one page for each chapter for the space taken up by the chapter opener and the empty portion of the page on the last chapter of the book.
3. If the chapters are to always start on a right hand page, divide the number of chapters by two and add the result into the count.

The counts we use for this purpose are 2,400 characters per full page for a 6" x 9" book, and 2,000 characters for a 5-1/2" x 8-1/2" book. Here's an example castoff for a novel with the relevant calculations:

Book Characteristics	
Manuscript character count:	496,000
Page size:	5-1/2" x 8-1/2"
Rule of thumb characters per page:	2,000
Chapters:	13

Castoff		
Element	**Pages**	**Comments**
Bastard title page	1	
Blank	1	
Title page	1	
Copyright page	1	
Dedication	1	
Blank	1	
Chapters	248	Calculate text pages by dividing character count by characters-per-page: 496,000 ÷ 2,000 = 248
Chapter opens/ends	13	
Chapters start right	7	If all chapters start right, assume half end on blank page.
Blank	1	
Blank	1	
Author note	1	
Blank	1	
Colophon	1	
Total est. pages	280	

By the way, you should always round *up* when a castoff calculation results in a decimal fraction rather than *down*. It is much better to be surprised by a lower page count for the final book—and therefore lower printing cost —than a higher page count!

CASTOFF METHOD 2: USE A CHARACTERS-PER-PAGE VALUE BASED ON TYPOGRAPHIC DATA

This method is very similar to the Rule of Thumb method, but instead of using a generic per-page character count, the per-page character count is based on the spatial characteristics of an actual typeface.

As is generally known, type is measured not in inches, but in picas and points. A point is 1/72", and a pica is 12 points. The "point size" of a typeface is not a precise guide to how big the letterforms actually are. As suggested above, letters of ten point Helvetica, for instance, take up about 16 percent more horizontal space than ten point letters of Adobe Janson. The better measure of how much space a typeface takes up is its Characters Per Pica (CPP) for a given point size. The CPP values are averages. With the CPP of a typeface and the measurements of the area taken up by type on the page—aka "type page"—you can get a pretty good estimate of how many characters will fit on a full page. A tech-savvy type house in Massachusetts, Technologies and Typography, has CPP values for many typefaces on its website (https://www.tekntype.com/tntfonts/).

A type page for a novel with a 5-1/2" x 8-1/2" page might be 25 picas wide by 36 picas high. You want to find out how many characters of 12-point Adobe Garamond set with line spacing of 14 points will fit on this page. First let's figure out how many lines of type will fit on a type page 34 picas high:

36 picas x 12 points per pica = 432 points
432 points / 14 points linespacing = 31 lines of type

Then let's figure out how many characters per line on a 25-pica line with 12-point Adobe Garamond, which has a CPP of 2.37:

2.37 x 25 = 59 characters per line on average

Then, to get the number of characters per full page:

31 lines of type x 59 characters per line = 1,829 characters per page

Now, let's revisit the castoff we created using the rule of thumb characters-per-page value:

Book Characteristics		
Manuscript character count:	496,000	
Page size:	5-1/2" x 8-1/2"	
Calculated characters per page:	1,829	(2.37 CPP x 25 pica line length) X 31 lines per page = 1,829 characters per page
Chapters:	13	

Castoff		
Element	**Pages**	**Comments**
Bastard title page	1	
Blank	1	
Title page	1	
Copyright page	1	
Dedication	1	
Blank	1	
Chapters	271	Calculate text pages by dividing character count by characters-per-page: 496,000 ÷ 1,829 = 271
Chapter opens/ends	13	
Chapters start right	7	If all chapters start right, assume half end on blank page.
Blank	1	
Blank	1	
Author note	1	
Blank	1	
Colophon	1	
Total est. pages	303	

INCORPORATING OTHER BOOK ELEMENTS IN THE CASTOFF

Illustrations

Illustrations are typically sized as the book is designed, so the number of pages they take up cannot be calculated directly. Instead, use an average of pages per illustration to estimate the pages taken up by the illustrations. This is easy if you are devoting a full page to each illustration:

24 Illustrations @ 1 per page = 24 pages

More likely the illustrations will not take up a full page on average. In our experience about 66% of a page per illustration is a good rule-of-thumb average if the illustrations are running within the text; for some reason illustrations always take up more than you expect if you size them so they are not tiny. The need to allow room for captions probably contributes to this. So the line on the list of elements would look like this:

15 illustrations @ 66% page per illustration = 10 pages

Inserts

Sometimes, illustrations are printed in sections bound into the text pages rather than running with the text. These sections are often printed on a coated paper while the text is printed on uncoated paper. The coated paper allows for better reproduction of photos and artwork. In digital book printing, inserts can have as few as two pages; with offset printing inserts page counts are usually in multiples of eight, because offset presses print on large sheets which are then folded into signatures containing even numbers of pages.

In a castoff, typically the insert page count is specified based on the number of illustrations and the average space factor for each:

15 illustrations and one blank = 16 pages

or

15 illustrations @ 50% page per illustration = 8 pages

There is usually a bit of trickiness in laying out inserts unless each image is given a full page, because images with a vertical aspect ratio cry out for a full page, while horizontals fit more neatly two to a page.

Tables

Because they can vary so widely in size tables are best listed individually in a castoff with an estimated space guesstimate assigned to each:

Table	Book Pages
Table 1	0.50
Table 2	1.00
Table 3	0.33
Table 4	2.50
Table 5	0.50
Table 6	0.50
Total	5.33
Round up to	6.00

Notes and Other Backmatter

As these are typically set in smaller type, each of them should be calculated separately and added to the total page count. Reasonable rule-of-thumb characters per page values for notes are 3,000 characters for a 5-1/2" x 8-1/2" page and 3,500 for a 6" x 9" page.

Indexes

Indexes do not lend themselves to page calculations because they are mostly white space. Assign them 8-20 pages in the castoff depending on how long the book is.

CONCLUSION

For a simple one-column book, it shouldn't take too long to use one of the castoff methods listed above. For more complicated books—those with lots of text, lots of chapters, lots of illustrations—it can take hours to do a proper castoff. Whether you want to invest the time depends on how important it is to you to get a relatively accurate printing cost estimate early in the project. It is those more complicated books for which printing costs can easily skyrocket, however, so if you are concerned about the budget, it is probably worth your time. Also, there are benefits other than just minimizing risk: doing the castoff is an excellent way to really think about and understand the bones of the book as you commence design and production.

APPENDIX B: PRINTING AND PUBLISHING SERVICES

Below are some resources for finding design, printing, distribution, and eBook services. These lists are partial—Internet searches will point you to many additional options. Just do your homework to ensure you're not trusting your project to an incompetent or fly-by-night operation. And remember cheaper is NOT always better; make sure you consider all the true costs involved (such as your time and sanity).

BOOK DESIGN

Google "Book design services" and you'll find companies that offer a range of publishing services, including book design. But if you're just want to find a freelance designer, below are some resources.

PUBLISHING PROFESSIONALS NETWORK

https://pubpronetwork.org/providers/
Maintains a directory of freelance book designers, editors, proofreaders, indexers, eBook converters, and more.

GRAPHIC ARTISTS GUILD

https://graphicartistsguild.org/guild-members-portfolios/
Allows you to browse portfolios of members, including designers, illustrators, and photographers.

DEXIGNER

https://www.dexigner.com/directory/cat/Book-Design/Designers
Maintains a directory of freelance book designers.

BOOK PRINTING, EBOOK CREATION, FULFILLMENT, AND DISTRIBUTION

Many companies offer both print and eBook publishing services, but most

BOOKMOBILE

https://bookmobile.com/
Provides short-run digital printing (SRDP), fulfillment, and distribution services

EBOOK CREATION, FULFILLMENT, AND DISTRIBUTION

BLURB

www.blurb.com
Blurb offers both POD (print-on-demand) printing services and eBook services, but since we strongly recommend against POD for print books, we suggest them here just as an eBook creator and aggregator.

BOOKBABY.COM AND OTHERS

APPENDIX C: CROWDFUNDING WEBSITES THAT SUPPORT PUBLISHING PROJECTS

Crowdfunding platforms spring to life, morph, and die out as quickly as anything else on the Internet, but below is a listing of those that may be of most interest currently to creators undertaking publishing projects (at least as of the publication of this book). We've included proven crowdfunding juggernauts with dedicated publishing categories, as well as interesting startups aimed specifically at writers and would-be publishers.

KICKSTARTER (HTTPS://WWW.KICKSTARTER.COM/)

With a focus on creative projects and a dedicated publishing category, Kickstarter is the largest crowdfunding platform in operation, claiming almost $3 billion pledged by over 13 million people to launch over 123,000 successful campaigns. Of the nearly 37,000 publishing projects that have been launched, just over 30 percent have been successful. Funding through Kickstarter is all-or-nothing: If the goal isn't reached, backers aren't charged. If a project is successful, Kickstarter charges a 5% fee on all the funds collected, plus a 3 to 5 percent payment processing fee.

INDIEGOGO (HTTPS://WWW.INDIEGOGO.COM/)

Indiegogo claims more than $1 billion in funds raised for over 650,000 projects. Indiegogo uses a fee structure comparable to Kickstarter but also offers an option to keep all funds raised even if the goal is not met. With a broader focus than Kickstarter, its writing and publishing category comprises a smaller subset of its campaigns, and unlike Kickstarter it doesn't offer any review or approval process before campaigns go live.

PUBLISHIZER (HTTPS://PUBLISHIZER.COM/)

Publishizer describes itself as "a book pre-orders platform that matches authors with publishers." Authors submit a proposal and, once it's approved, launch a campaign with the aim of capturing as many pre-orders as possible. Publishizer queries potential publishers (including traditional publishers, hybrid publishers, and service publishers) and fields any offers that the author receives. Publishizer charges a whopping 30 percent fee on all preorders processed through their site along with a 15 percent "agent fee" for paid advances and future royalties, in some cases.

PUBLAUNCH (HTTPS://WWW.PUBLAUNCH.COM/)

Set to launch its full site in 2017, PubLaunch is currently available in beta and combines traditional crowdfunding for publishing projects along with a marketplace designed to connect authors to publishing services. Authors upload a manuscript, select the services in which they're interested, get an estimate for what those services will cost from PubLaunch's suppliers, then crowdfund to raise the needed funds. Fees are comparable to Kickstarter and Indiegogo.

UNBOUND (U.K.; HTTPS://UNBOUND.COM/)

Claiming 218 successful projects, Unbound acts as a publisher for projects that reach their fundraising goal through the website. Authors submit a pitch and, if it's accepted, launch a crowdfunding campaign and promote their book. Unbound determines the publication costs, and if the necessary amount is raised, handles the publication (including editing, design, and printing). Any post-publication profit from sales is split 50/50 by Unbound and the author.

INKSHARES (HTTPS://WWW.INKSHARES.COM/)

Like Unbound, Inkshares is a hybrid publisher and crowdfunding platform. With 156 funded titles, their process, services, and fees are comparable to Unbound.

PATREON (HTTPS://WWW.PATREON.COM/)

Patreon is a crowdfunding platform that uses a subscription model, where backers (or patrons) make ongoing contributions to creators, either as regularly recurring payments or per work of art published. Patreon charges a 5 percent fee on all pledges, plus a 3 to 5 percent payment processing fee, and claims its creators have collectively raised over $100,000,000 since its 2013 inception. The platform has a dedicated writing category.

APPENDIX D: BINDING SPECIFICS

HOW PAPERBACKS ARE BOUND

- The interior pages of the book are printed and gathered together into a book block consisting either of loose pages or folded groups of pages called signatures.
- The cover is printed and, typically, laminated for protection. At this point it is a flat sheet.
- In the binding machine:

  a. The covers are stacked upside down in a feeder.
  b. The book blocks are inserted in a clamp one by one.
  c. The clamp moves the book block through the binder across stations where the spine is milled to prepare it for glue, and hot liquid glue is rolled across the spine.
  d. The clamp moves the book block over a nipping station where the upside down cover waits, positioned precisely on a steel platen.
  e. The platen raises to press the cover against the glue-covered spine and simultaneously closes to fold the front and back covers around the book block. The clamp pauses to allow the glue to cool and set a bit.
  f. The newly covered book block travels to a delivery chute, where the clamp releases it.

- The book is trimmed on three sides: the top, foreedge and bottom.
- The book is packed in a carton with other copies of the same book.
- This process is called "perfect binding." The two kinds of glue that are widely used for perfect binding are Ethylene-vinyl acetate (EVA) and Polyurethane reactive (PUR). Both are heated before application to the spine of the book.

WHICH PAPERBACK GLUE TO SPECIFY

In general, EVA is perfectly adequate for binding books on normal weight, uncoated paper stocks. PUR creates a stronger bond when binding coated stocks, heavy stocks, and pages printed on some digital color printers (e.g., the Xerox iGen). These printers use large amounts of silicone oil when printing, and EVA glues do not like to stick when silicone oil is present. PUR is also used in the school library market, where binding durability is critical. As a side note, some digital printing companies recommend printing color illustrated books on high-quality, heavy uncoated stocks because they can then be bound strongly with EVA glue, as well as because digital presses print better on uncoated rather than coated stock.

BINDING GLUES COMPARED

Glue type	Strength with uncoated papers	Strength with coated papers	Flexibility	Cost
EVA	Excellent	Poor	Good	Low
PUR	Excellent	Excellent	Excellent	Premium

SEWN PAPERBACKS

Occasionally, publishers request that paperback books be Smythe-sewn before being perfect bound. Because the perfect binding still uses glue–whether EVA or PUR–the book will have the same qualities as a regular perfect-bound book. The durability depends more on how well the binding was done than on whether the book block is sewn. In other words, this belt-and-suspenders approach is a waste of money.

HOW HARDCOVERS ARE BOUND

- The interior pages of the book are printed and gathered together into a book block consisting of loose pages or folded signatures.
- The pages (or folded signatures) are attached at the spine with glue, sometimes with a reinforcing strip of muslin.
- A folded sheet called an endsheet is glued onto the first page of the book block, and one on the last page.
- A case is custom-made for the book.
- The front endsheet is glued to the inside of the front case cover, and the back endsheet glued to the inside of the back case cover. The glue floods the whole area of the endsheet and inside covers, creating a very strong bond.
- The whole assembly is clamped so that the glue sets it into a nice, tight book.
- If there is a dust jacket, it is wrapped around the book.
- The book is packed into a carton with other copies of the same book.

KEY HARDCOVER BINDING OPTIONS

There are many options for hardcover binding involving colors, textures and other aesthetic aspects of the materials used. The key production consideration, however, is how the book block is assembled. Here are some common methods:

- The book block is perfect bound with endsheet material as a cover, using EVA or PUR glue. This is sometimes called "adhesive casebinding."
- The book block is glued up using cold glue in a process called "adhesive fan binding."
- When the pages are printed on large sheets and folded into signatures, the signatures can be sewn together into a book block. This is called "Smythe sewing."
- Signatures or pages can be "side-stitched." This only works for books with lower page counts (e.g., children's picture books).

APPENDIX E: BUDGET WORKSHEETS

TITLE P&L, MODIFIED FOR A KICKSTARTER PROJECT

For free worksheets, email kickstart@bookmobile.com with "Free Worksheets" in the subject line.

TITLE P&L, MODIFIED FOR A KICKSTARTER PROJECT, WITH DISTRIBUTION TO BOOK STORES

For free worksheets, email kickstart@bookmobile.com with "Free Worksheets" in the subject line.

Title P&L Modified for a Kickstarter Book Publishing Project

Created by Don Leeper, Bookmobile

Enter Data In Yellow Cells
Green Cells Are Automatically Calculated

BOOK INFORMATION

Title:	Palfrey's Glen – Sample P&L
List price:	$45.00
Printing, per book:	$25.00
Postage, per book:	$2.65
Fulfillment, per book:	$2.00

BOOK SALES MODEL

BOOK SALES

	Copies	Shipments	Price	Discount	Selling price	Extension
Copies sold to individuals	200	0	$45.00	0.00%	$45.00	$9,000.00
Shipping and handling charged to individuals	0	200	5.00	0.00%	5.00	1,000.00
Copies for backers	600	0	35.00	100.00%	0.00	0.00
Shipping and handling charged for backers	0	600	5.00	100.00%	0.00	0.00
Copies for project team members	20	0	35.00	100.00%	0.00	0.00
	820	800				$10,000.00
	Total copies	Total ships				Total sales $

BOOK PROFIT & LOSS PROJECTION

		Units	Cost/unit	Totals
INCOME				
	Book sales income (from Book Sales, above)			$10,000.00
	Kickstarter funding			24,000.00
	Less Kickstarter fee (5%)			-1,200.00
	Less card processing fee (4%)			-960.00
			TOTAL INCOME	$31,840.00
VARIABLE COSTS		**Units**	**Cost/unit**	**Totals**
	Printing, books sold	200	25.00	$5,000.00
	Printing, backer and team copies	620	25.00	$15,500.00
	Shipping, books sold	200	2.65	530.00
	Shipping, backer copies	600	2.65	1,590.00
	Fulfillment services	800	2.00	1,600.00
	Credit card fees on sales at 3%			400.00
			TOTAL VARIABLE COSTS	24,620.00
			GROSS MARGIN	$7,220.00
PROJECT EXPENSES				
	Development			
	Editorial		250.00	
	Artwork		50.00	
	Cover design		700.00	
	Text design and layout		1,100.00	
	Printing setup charges		120.00	
	Travel		50.00	
	Equipment rental		50.00	
		Total Development		2,320.00
	Marketing and Promotion			
	Project website		500.00	
	Copy writing		125.00	
	Launch party		400.00	
	Miscellaneous		200.00	
		Total Marketing and Promotion		1,225.00
	Fundraising			
	Video – script		400.00	
	Video – production		1,000.00	
	Still photography		400.00	
	Copy writing		250.00	
		Total Fundraising		2,050.00
	Professional Services			
	Legal		1,000.00	
	Bookkeeping & Accounting		200.00	
	Tax preparation		200.00	
		Total Professional Services		1,400.00
			TOTAL PROJECT EXPENSES	6,995.00
			PROJECT SURPLUS (SHORTFALL)	$225.00

Title P&L Modified for a Kickstarter Book Publishing Project, With Distribution to Bookstores

Created by Don Leeper, Bookmobile

Enter Data In Yellow Cells
Green Cells Are Automatically Calculated

BOOK INFORMATION

Title:	Palfrey's Glen – Sample P&L
List price:	$45.00
Copies printed	2,500
Printing, per book:	$12.00
Postage, per book:	$2.65
Fulfillment, per book:	$2.00

BOOK SALES MODEL

BOOK SALES—DIRECT AND BACKERS

	Copies	Shipments	Price	Discount	Selling price	Extension
Copies sold to individuals	200	0	$45.00	0.00%	$45.00	$9,000.00
Shipping and handling charged to individuals	0	200	5.00	0.00%	5.00	1,000.00
Copies for backers	800	0	45.00	100.00%	0.00	0.00
Shipping and handling charged for backers	0	800	0.00	100.00%	0.00	0.00
Copies for project team members	20	0	45.00	100.00%	0.00	0.00
	1020	1000			Total direct sales	$10,000.00
	Total copies	Total ships				

BOOK SALES—TO BOOK TRADE

	Copies	Shipments	Price	Discount	Selling price	Extension
Copies sold to wholesalers and Amazon	750	0	$45.00	55.00%	$20.25	$15,187.50
Shipping charged to wholesalers	0	750	0.00	0.00%	0.00	0.00
Copies sold to retailers	250	0	45.00	40.00%	27.00	6,750.00
Shipping charged to retailers	0	250	0.50	0.00%	0.50	125.00
	1000	1000				$22,062.50
	Total copies	Total ships			Less allowance for returns (35%)	-$7,721.88
					Trade sales net of returns	$14,340.63
					Less distributor fee (20%)	-$2,868.13
					Net trade revenue to publisher (you)	$11,472.50
Grand Totals	2020	2000			TOTAL BOOK SALES	$21,472.50
	Books	Shipments				

BOOK PROFIT & LOSS PROJECTION

INCOME

Book sales income (from Book Sales, above)	$21,472.50
Kickstarter funding	24,000.00
Less Kickstarter fee (5%)	-1,200.00
Less card processing fee (4%)	-960.00
TOTAL INCOME	$43,312.50

VARIABLE COSTS

	Units	Cost/unit	Totals
Shipping, direct sales and backer copies	1000	2.65	2,650.00
Fulfillment services, direct sales and backer copies	1000	2.00	2,000.00
Credit card fees on direct sales at 4%			400.00
TOTAL VARIABLE COSTS			5,050.00
GROSS MARGIN			$38,262.50

PROJECT EXPENSES

	Units	Cost/unit	
Development			
Editorial		250.00	
Artwork		50.00	
Cover design		700.00	
Text design and layout		1,100.00	
Printing setup charges		120.00	
Travel		50.00	
Equipment rental		50.00	
Total Development			2,320.00
Printing			
Printing, all books	2500	12.00	30,000.00
Freight to warehouse	1	400.00	400.00
Trade distribution setup and expenses			
Trade distribution setup and expenses	1	500.00	500.00
Warehouse fees for 12 monthes	12	30.00	360.00
Marketing and Promotion			
Project website		500.00	
Copy writing		125.00	
Launch party		400.00	
Miscellaneous		200.00	
Total Marketing and Promotion			1,225.00
Fundraising			
Video – script		400.00	
Video – production		1,000.00	
Still photography		400.00	
Copy writing		250.00	
Total Fundraising			2,050.00
Professional Services			
Legal		1,000.00	
Bookkeeping & Accounting		200.00	
Tax preparation		200.00	
Total Professional Services			1,400.00
TOTAL PROJECT EXPENSES			38,255.00
PROJECT SURPLUS (SHORTFALL)			$7.50

APPENDIX F: PREPARING FULL-COLOR IMAGES FOR PRINTING

BACKGROUND

The core issue with printing any image file is that displaying a color image on a computer screen is fundamentally different than printing the same image on paper. Computers represent color in the RGB (Red-Green-Blue) color scheme. In all but very rare instances, commercial presses print color using the CMYK (Cyan-Magenta-Yellow-Black) color scheme. This means that when you print an image on a commercial press, every point of color in an image that is represented on your computer by combining red, green, and blue in various intensities must be transformed into a combination of cyan, magenta, yellow, and black inks. Because the range of colors that can be created on a good RGB monitor—its color "gamut"—is larger than the CMYK printing ink gamut, there are colors that you can represent in RGB that are not reproducible by a combination of cyan, magenta, yellow, and black. Consequently, the transformation is not as simple as converting each RGB color to the same color generated with CMYK. Instead, RGB colors that fall *outside* the CMYK gamut must be converted to different color *within* the CMYK gamut. How you make that transformation can make a big difference in how an image prints. The fact that the CMYK gamut is not as large as the RGB gamut doesn't mean you can't produce printed images of the highest quality. It just means that you must work within the limitations of the CMYK medium.

Besides the issue of differing RGB and CMYK gamuts, viewing an image on a computer screen and viewing it on a printed page differ in another important respect: one *adds* colors to arrive at the colors you perceive, the other *subtracts* color to arrive at the color you perceive. A color monitor emits the viewing light itself and makes colors by adding together different intensities of red, green and blue. An image on a printed page is viewed quite differently. Unlike a monitor, the page itself produces no light: the viewing light is whatever the ambient light is—a warm incandescent lamp, a fluorescent lamp, sunlight from a window, or, often, a combination of sources. The ambient light passes through the translucent ink on the page, reflects off the paper back through the ink, and enters your eye. The light that hits your eye consists of those parts of the spectrum that were not filtered out—*subtracted*—by the ink, not as in the case of an RGB, the colors that were *added* by the red, green and blue light-emitting phosphors on the screen. Which is why the RGB system is called additive and the CMYK system subtractive.

Besides the variability of the ambient lighting, the paper itself affects the colors ultimately perceived. What is called "white" paper actually varies from paper type to paper type, and even from mill lot to mill lot within the same brand and type of paper. Some "white" papers have a warm tint to them, others a cool bluish tint. In either case, the tint of the paper shifts the colors perceived as the ambient light reflects off of it.

STEP 1

The first step in the process of having your images print the way you want is to emulate the CMYK gamut on your computer screen by 1) calibrating your monitor and 2) using the CMYK color profile to "soft proof" the images, so you can get an idea of how they are going to print.

Before we look at this in detail, be aware that not all programs you might use to make book pages allow you to do CMYK soft proofing. In these examples we use the industry standard software tools: Adobe Photoshop for image editing and Adobe InDesign for page layout, both of which allow soft proofing with CMYK profiles. But before that you need to calibrate your monitor.

CALIBRATING YOUR MONITOR

Calibrating your monitor sets the intensity and RGB color representations to standard profiles so that when you soft proof with a color profile, the profile can accurately adjust the viewing colors. All monitors vary, even monitors of the same make and model, so calibration is essential. The best way to calibrate is to use a tool like the Datacolor Spyder5PRO or the x-rite ColorMunki. (There are other brands as well: check reviews.) Calibrators start at about $90, so they are not terribly expensive. These tools are hung over the monitor so that the calibrator's sensors are right up against the screen. The included calibration software generates colors on the screen, the sensor measures the colors, and then the software creates a profile that automatically adjusts the screen colors to standard settings. It will probably take about an hour the first time you calibrate. One further note about calibration: as with viewing printed pages, ambient light matters. See the calibrator instructions for the manufacturer's recommendations for adjusting ambient lighting.

SOFT PROOFING

Now that you've calibrated your monitor, you can use a CMYK color profile to previsualize—aka soft proof—how your images are going to print. Many printing companies use GRACol2013, a standard sheetfed offset press CMYK profile. Because its often installed by default, I'm going to use it in my examples. If it is not installed on your computer you can find it here, along with a SWOP profile, which you don't need unless your book will be printed on a web offset press (which is highly unlikely).

Your printer may have a custom profile for you to use to better match their particular press setup. If they do, they should also provide instructions on how to install the supplied profile on your computer.

Here are the steps to soft proof in Photoshop.

First, set up your "Working CMYK" environment:

1. Go to Edit / Color Settings.
2. At the very top beside "Settings:" select "Custom."
3. Set the options you see as follows:

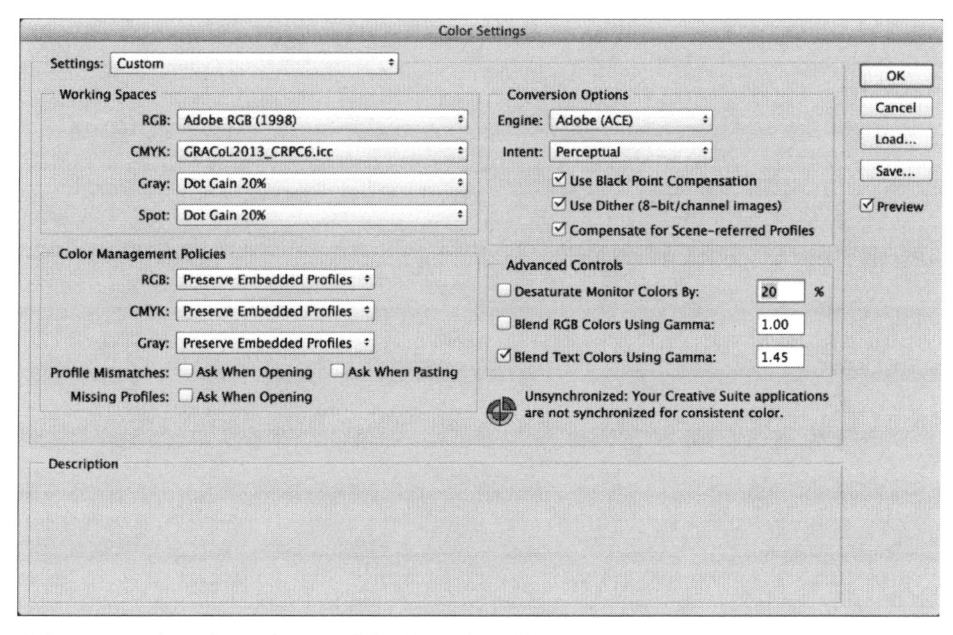

Color settings for soft proofing in Adobe Photoshop CC.

Now open an image and set up viewing for soft proofing:

1. Go to View / Proof Setup.
2. Select "Working CMYK."

Now you can toggle between straight RGB viewing and Soft Proofing with the CMYK proof setup by selecting View / Proof Color, or on a Mac, Command-Y.

Another handy tool is the Gamut Warning, toggled with View / Gamut Warning. The Gamut Warning setting displays in gray those areas where the RGB colors are outside the CMYK gamut, as shown in the image below. Those are the areas you need to pay attention to when you're adjusting the image for printing in CMYK.

Screen captures of Photoshop session:

LEFT-HAND PANEL: *Regular RGB view. (View / Proof Color toggled off.)*

MIDDLE PANEL: *CMYK Soft Proof view, rendered with Perceptual intent. (View / Proof Color toggled on.) Note how the blues in the sky have been shifted to bring them within the CMYK gamut.*

RIGHT-HAND PANEL: *RGB view with gamut warning. (View / Gamut Warning toggled on.) The gray shading indicates areas of the RGB image that are outside of the CMYK gamut as defined in the GRACol2013 profile.*

To use CMYK soft proofing in InDesign, you follow essentially the same steps outlined above. You can find additional information on the Adobe website (https://help.adobe.com/en_US/creativesuite/cs/using/WS3F71DA01-0962-4b2e-B7FD-C956F8659BB3.html).

ADJUSTING COLOR FOR CMYK

Because soft proofing gives you an idea of how your image will print on a CMYK press, you can use it to adjust the image on screen until it is optimized for CMYK reproduction. The color profile itself can do part of this, if you choose the right RGB-CMYK conversion method. There are basically two conversion methods—called conversion "Intents" in Adobe software—for converting RGB colors are that of potential use for photographers: *relative colorimetric* and *perceptual.*

Relative Colorimetric Conversion

During conversion, specifying relative colorimetric intent does two things:

- RGB colors that fall *within* the CMYK gamut are mapped one-for-one to the corresponding CMYK color.
- RGB colors that are *outside* the CMYK gamut are mapped to the nearest color available in the CMYK color space.

Perceptual Conversion

Instead of converting all the RGB colors outside the CMYK gamut to colors at the boundaries of the CMYK color space, the perceptual conversion method adjusts the entire range of RGB colors in a gradation—both those inside and those outside the CMYK gamut—so the all fit smoothly within the CMYK gamut.

Example

Let's say a photograph has an area of blue sky in it. Like all real images, the sky has many gradations of blue because of changes between the zenith and the horizon, atmospheric factors like the edges of clouds, and so on. It is likely that many of the blues in a piece of sky can be represented in RGB, but not all of them can be reproduced in CMYK.

Using the **relative colorimetric** conversion method, all of the RGB blues outside the CMYK gamut will be mapped to the closest CMYK value at the boundary of the CMYK color space, and will map the colors which are already inside the CMYK gamut to their CMYK exact equivalent. This means all the detail represented in the RGB blue gradations that were originally outside the CMYK gamut are lost, resulting in areas of a flat, single color, unrealistic sky. This in turn will also likely create banding in the sky.

Using the **perceptual** conversion method adjusts the entire range of colors in a gradation—both those originally inside the CMYK gamut and those originally outside the CMYK gamut—in order to preserve the gradation present in the RGB image. The result is that at any point in the blue sky of the image the CMYK colors will likely *not* match the RGB colors exactly, but the image is better than when converted with the relative colorimetric method because the gradation itself is not lost.

The upshot of all this is that when specifying the rendering intent for RGB to CMYK conversion—both for soft proofing and for creating PDFs for the printer—you should choose the perceptual option.

While using the perceptual conversion method does a lot of the heavy lifting in terms of rendering an RGB image into CMYK, for some images you may want to use the various tools within Photoshop—curves, levels, and so on—to optimize the image appearance when viewed with the CMYK color profile. Just as when a photographer adjusts a newly-converted RAW image fresh out of the camera, there is a lot of potential to improve the image here, as long as you think of CMYK printing as a medium in itself, and not as a way to match exactly colors seen on an RGB monitor.

STEP 2

It's crucial to make sure that all PDF settings are correct for your color images to translate properly to print. This requires three things: 1) load the appropriate color settings in InDesign, 2) load the PDF presets supplied by the printer, and finally 3) output the PDF file.

The images below show the Mac version of InDesign, but the Windows version is very similar.

LOADING THE COLOR SETTINGS

It is important that the correct color profile and other settings be set up in InDesign before creating PDFs with full-color images. The printer you are using should furnish an Adobe color settings file (.csf file), which will specify the correct color profile, either a standard profile like GRACoL or a custom profile for their particular press setup. It should be exactly the same profile you used for any soft proofing in Photoshop or InDesign. These examples use a .csf file referencing the Bookmobile custom ICC profile. Here's how to load the color settings in InDesign:

1. Go to Edit / Color Settings.

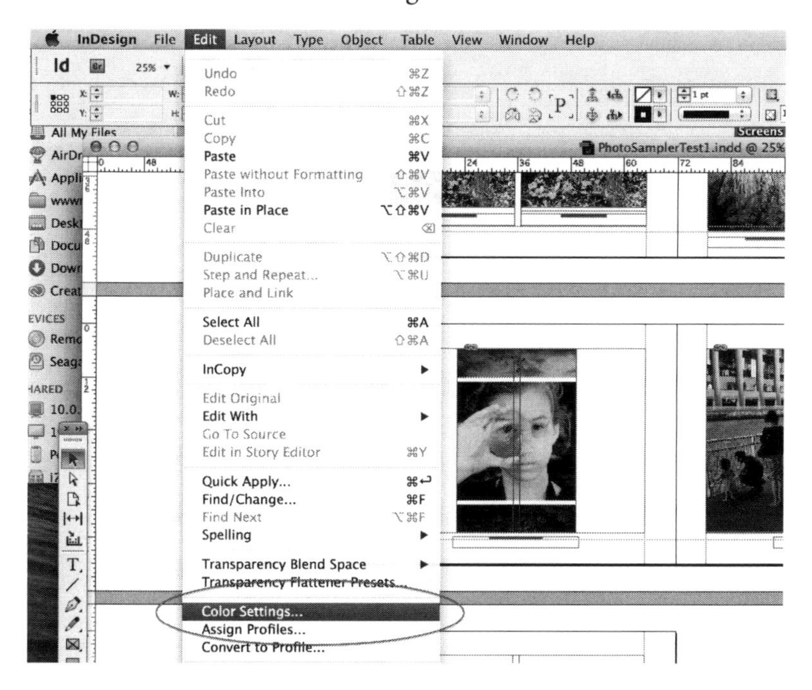

2. Click the Load button.

Color Settings

Unsynchronized: Your Creative Suite applications are not synchronized for consistent color. To synchronize, select Suite Color Settings in Bridge.

OK
Cancel
Load...
Save...

Settings: North America General Purpose 2

Advanced Mode

Working Spaces

RGB: sRGB IEC61966-2.1

CMYK: U.S. Web Coated (SWOP) v2

Color Management Policies

RGB: Preserve Embedded Profiles

CMYK: Preserve Numbers (Ignore Linked Profiles)

Profile Mismatches: Ask When Opening

Ask When Pasting

Missing Profiles: Ask When Opening

Description:

Position the pointer over a heading to view a description.

3. Find the color profile file, select it, and click Open.

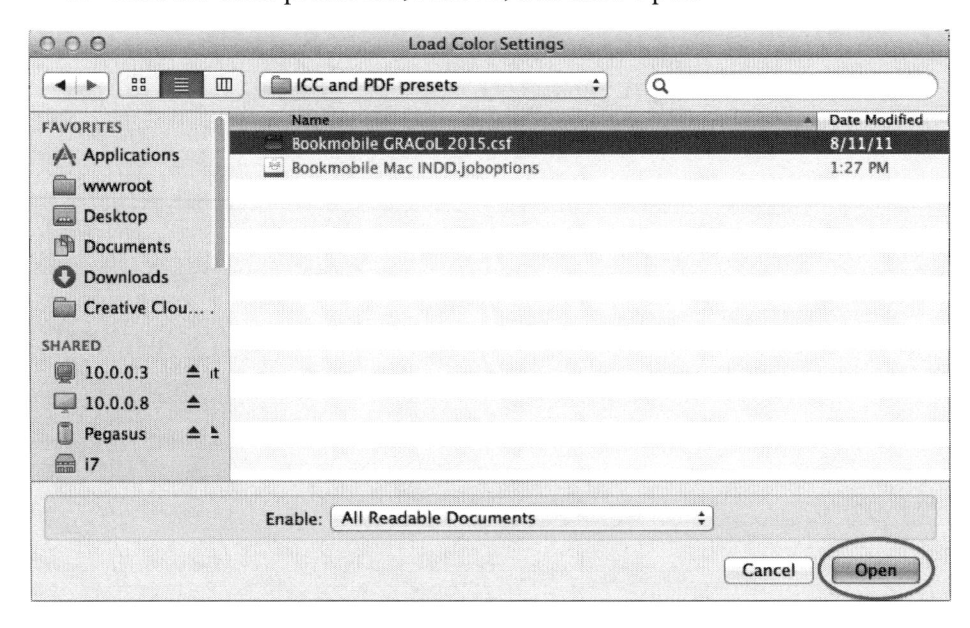

That's it for Color Settings! When you're done the Color Settings should look like this:

SET UP THE PDF PRESETS

Creating a PDF for high-quality printing requires paying attention to all the output settings—and there are a lot of them! Fortunately, most printers can provide a PDF presets file that will automatically set up InDesign to produce PDF files tuned for their production process. (If they don't provide a presets file, they should provide screen shots of all the appropriate settings so you can create a preset yourself.) Here's how to load a printer's PDF settings in InDesign:

1. Go to File / Adobe PDF Presets, and select Define.

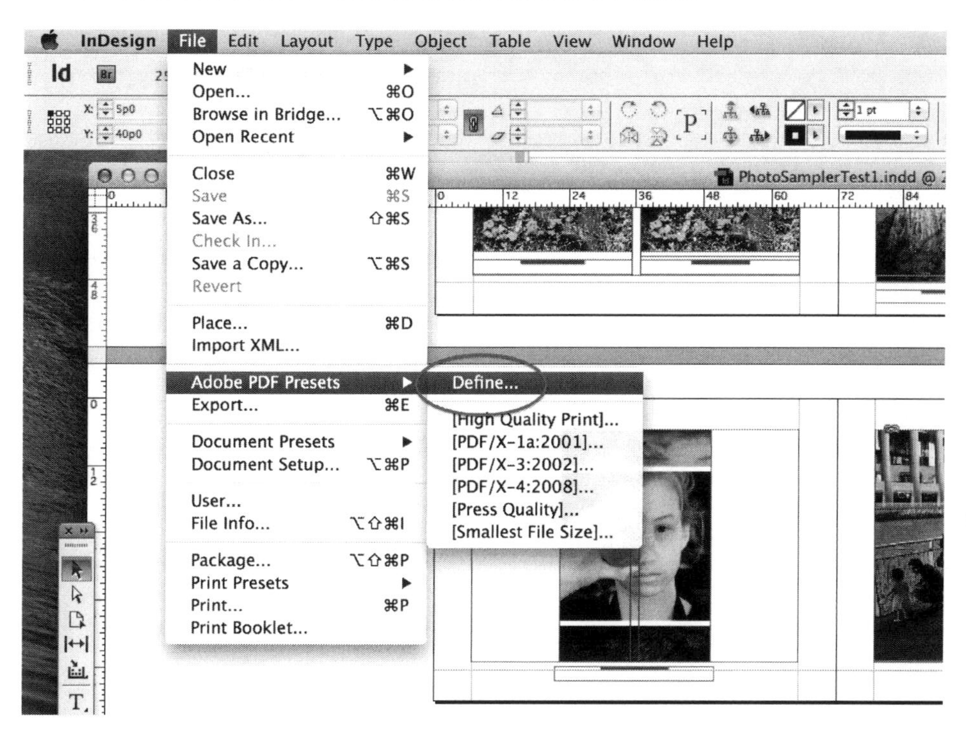

2. When the Adobe PDF Presets box comes up, click the Load button.

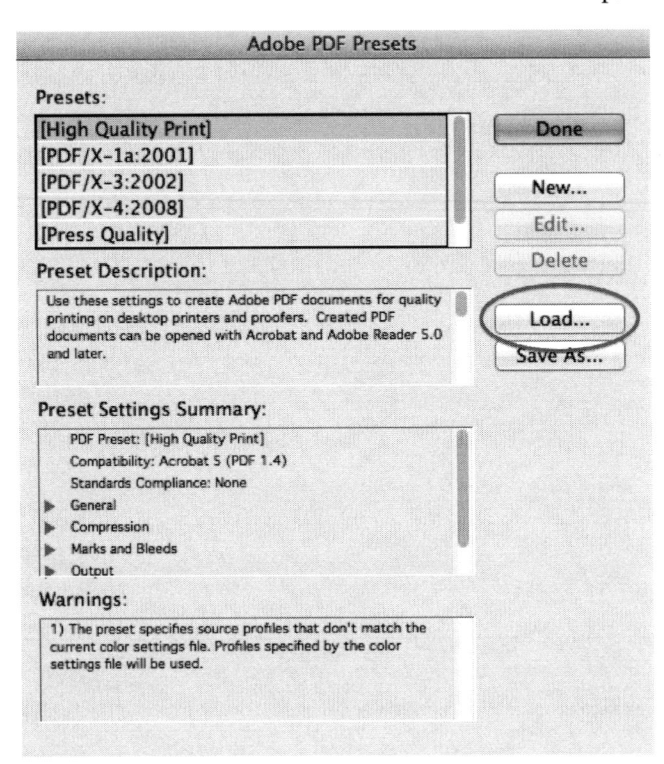

3. Locate the presets file supplied by the printer, select it, and click Open. That's it!

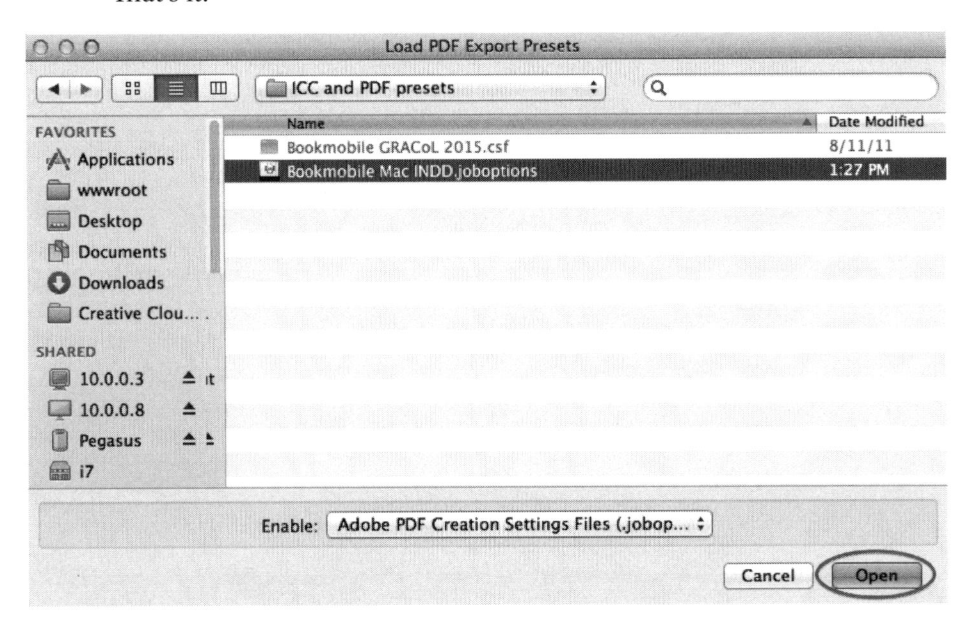

CREATING THE PDF

1. With your InDesign photo book file open, select the PDF preset you just loaded to use for output by going to File / Adobe PDF Presets. The preset you just loaded appears in the menu: select it.

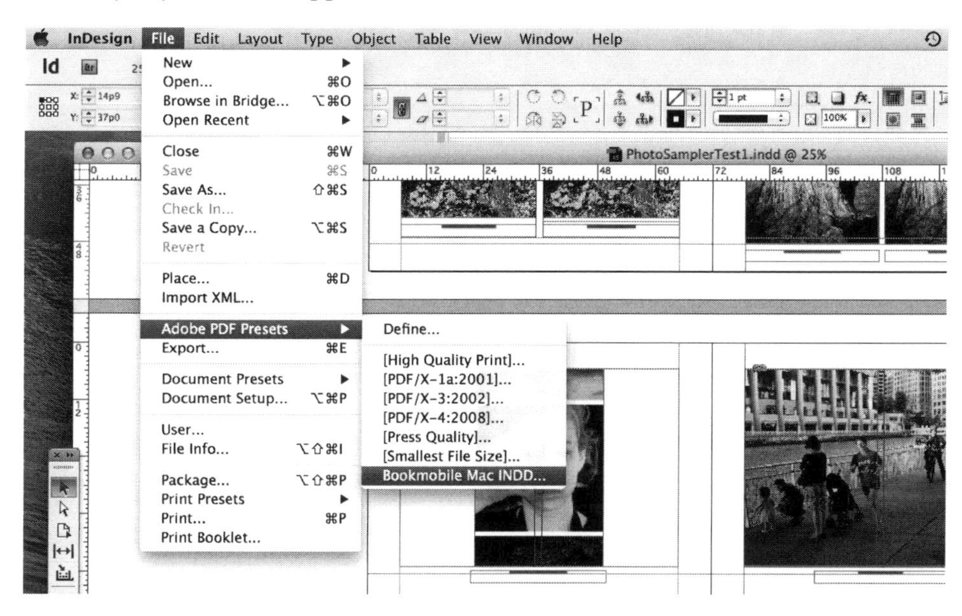

2. Name your output file and indicate where you want it to be saved. Then press Save.

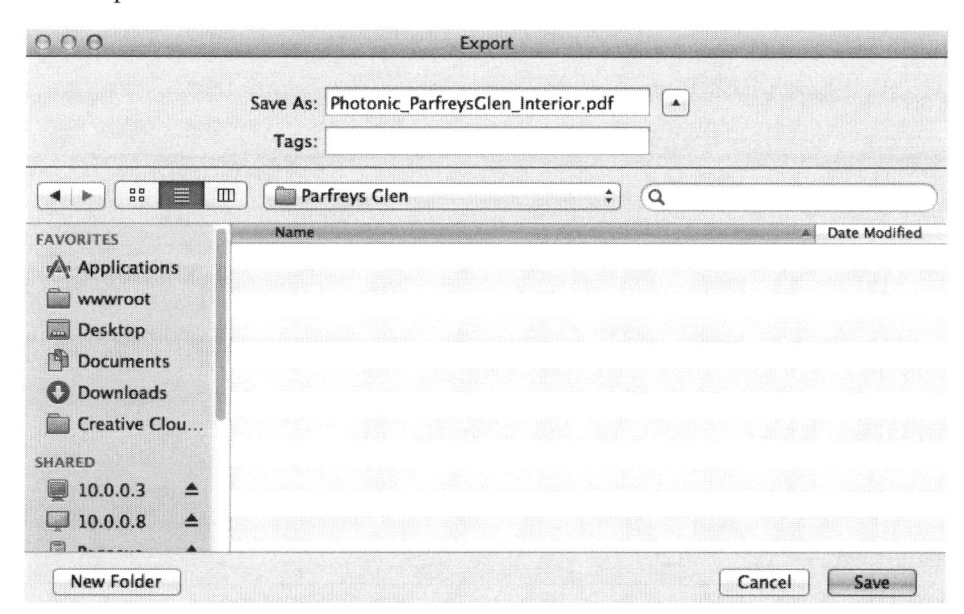

NOTE: it is a really good idea to name the file with the title of your book and description of the file, something like: MeanStreets_Interior.pdf, or MeanStreets_Cover.pdf. Adding the company name makes it bulletproof: Streetphoto_MeanStreetsInterior.pdf. Don't just use something like "book.pdf" or even "bookinterior.pdf": your printer is likely dealing with hundreds of book projects at a time: anything you can do to help keep things straight will be to your benefit.

3. Finally, click the Export button on the Export Adobe PDF screen.

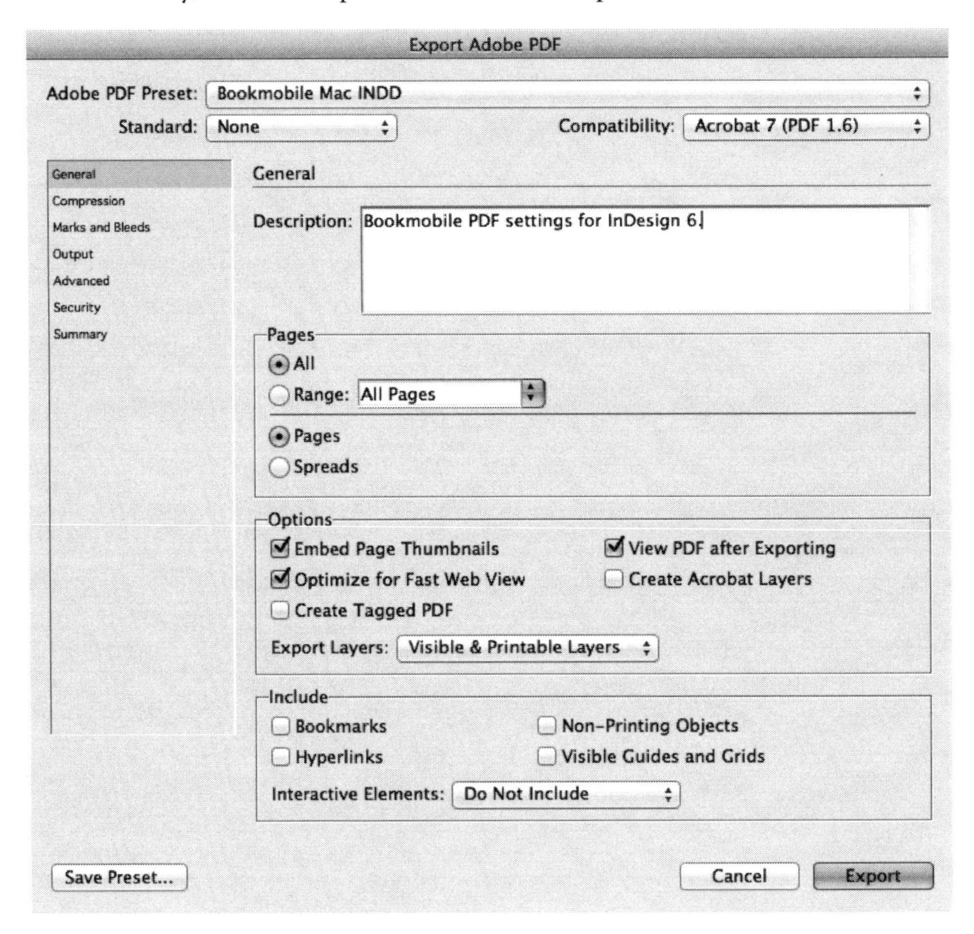

SENDING THE FILE TO THE PRINTER

Big hi-res PDF files cannot usually be sent by email. The printer will provide instructions on how to upload your file via FTP, Hightail, or other file transport method.

STEP 3

As we've noted, your RGB will not—cannot—look the same when transformed into a CMYK printed page. If you have gone through the drill of calibrating your monitor and soft proofing and prepared your PDF correctly you shouldn't have any major surprises when viewing your printed contract proofs or digital press proofs. However, this is where the rubber hits the road: this is where you are going to approve an offset contract proof or digital press proofs that the press operator will use as a guide for printing the actual book pages and cover.

Depending on your images, your CMYK proofs may look great right off the bat. Some kinds of images, however, are trickier. Images with pastel colors, for example, are notoriously tricky to convert and print in CMYK. Because they are made up of small amounts of color to begin with, slight shifts in the amounts of a single color—magenta or cyan in particular—can skew the pastel color dramatically. Pastels are going to require your attention on the proofs, and on the part of the press operator.

Choose a good place to review your proofs. Remember, it is the ambient light, filtered through the inks and reflected off the paper back through the ink, that determines the colors you actually see. The ambient light should be ample, and representative of where you expect your book to be viewed in terms of color temperature. Avoid nasty narrow spectrum fluorescents and dominant sunlight both.

Review each image individually. If it is OK, move on to the next one. To make changes or corrections you can either make them yourself in Photoshop and InDesign or have the printer do them. If you do them yourself and only a few pages are involved, you can output PDFs the affected pages individually to give to the printer: they are quite used to replacing individual pages. If a lot of pages are affected it might be more cost effective to output the whole book again. Ask the printer. In either case, it is super important to output any correction PDFs in exactly the same way you created the PDF the proof you just reviewed was made from: otherwise you will be starting over as far as reviewing proofs because the initial proof is no longer representative of what you have supplied.

If you want to have the printer make the changes, indicate any issues directly on the proof with a pen or marker. Indicate bad color shifts by saying "too red," "too purple," "too yellow," and so on. Only if you are an experienced CMYK prepress person or press operator would I recommend requesting specific changes like "-3% cyan in this area." It's like going to the doctor: you don't go in and say, “Doc, I’ve got pneumonia,” you say, “My lungs are wheezing and I’m feeling rotten.” Let the experts do the diagnosis. If images look fuzzy, write it directly on the proof. If shadow detail seems to have disappeared, write it on the proof, circling the area you’re concerned about. So as not to waste time, though, make sure that the original image wasn’t fuzzy to begin with and that the shadow detail is actually there in the first place. The printer can’t create detail where there was none to begin with.

INDEX

C

D

K

L

M

N

O

P

Q

R

S

T